DES HANNON

DES PUBLISHED POEM

PAGE 51

ANCHOR BOOKS

FP 2003 SERIES . . .
POEMS FROM THE NATION

Edited by

Rachael Radford

First published in Great Britain in 2003 by
ANCHOR BOOKS
Remus House,
Coltsfoot Drive,
Peterborough, PE2 9JX
Telephone (01733) 898102

HB ISBN 1 84418 120 0
SB ISBN 1 84418 121 9

FOREWORD

Anchor Books is a small press, established in 1992, with the aim of promoting readable poetry to as wide an audience as possible.

We hope to establish an outlet for writers of poetry who may have struggled to see their work in print.

The poems presented here have been selected from many entries, and as always editing proved to be a difficult task.

I trust this selection will delight and please the authors and all those who enjoy reading poetry.

Rachael Radford
Editor

CONTENTS

STARS

The stars are there forever
And now we're together,
Stay with me, for now and forever
And for as long as the stars are together.

Kenny Roxburgh

UNTITLED

Thank you for the respect you've shown
by keeping your appointment.
Thank you for being so nice to me,
making me feel so important.
Thank you for the plans we made,
one more promise that's not broken.
Thank you for your honesty,
no false words ever spoken.
Thank you for my self-esteem,
you've lifted me up high.
Thank you for being welcoming
and not saying goodbye.
Thank you for your trust in me,
not doubting my reaction.
And thank God for the most important thing,
my bitter-sweet sarcasm.

Nicola Sheehan

SHOPPING

Shopping with one's wife is a dementing thing,
With not a lot of money, they want everything.
Dragging us round clothes shops galore,
What do we know about silks and velour?
We hang about while they try on ten suits,
Three pairs of trousers and four pairs of boots.
We stand outside in the freezing rain,
Then they call us in to look. Oh, not again.
We stand outside having a smoke,
Forty cigs, we cough and choke,
Pockets full of half-smoked fags.
At the end of the day, they've not bought any rags,
But we have spent six pounds on two packets of fags.

B Harris

JODI

Daddy loves Jodi, all hearts and flowers.
He misses her so, he's counting the hours.
She wonders why he's not here anymore,
Oh why can't it be like it was before?
Daddy loves Jodi more than life, it's true,
Jodi doesn't know what Daddy goes through.
Beautiful Jodi, silky-haired, bubbly and fun,
Daddy loves Jodi, his little one.
Circumstances have torn them apart,
Jodi not aware that it's breaking his heart,
If only they could spend a week together.
But Jodi won't be a child forever -
One day, Jodi will use her own voice,
That's when Jodi will make her own choice.
Don't forget me Jodi, I'll keep in touch,
Daddy loves Jodi so very much.

Barbra Lee

HEARTFELT THANKS

I cry an ocean
When you're gone,
Stripped of my other
Blacked-out my sun,
Remembering thoughts
That I wanted to share,
Then look up from thinking
To see you're not there.
Soon, when the night comes
And day is done,
My heart starts to sing
For my baby must come
And I will be waiting,
Eternally yours,
With heartfelt love glowing,
Our spirits to soar.
How lucky I was
To find you and love
And to have a whole lifetime to share.
How happy you make me,
How safe and how warm,
I'm only complete when you're there.

Sarah Newell

To A Bully

I wish I knew your reasons, can you tell me why
It gave you so much pleasure to bully me 'til I'd cry?
Was I too small or fat or tall, was I too black or white?
Did I speak a foreign language, was I too dim or bright?
At any time of any day, not knowing what I'd done,
You'd seek me out, you'd find me, I'd be cornered with nowhere
                                                    to run.
You always walked off proud and tall, a hero to your friends,
While I was left to cower in terror, my nightmare would never end.
You were in my head when I went to bed and you even invaded
                                                    my dreams,
The bruises healed, they always did, but the real damage went deeper,
                                                    it seems.
I wonder who your victim is now, now that it's no longer me,
Is it your wife, or maybe your child? I just thank the Lord I am free.

June Briggs

SIGHTLESS EYES

Sightless eyes on a muddy bank,
Is there someone who really cares?
No one gathers to give their thanks,
Collared man mumbles prayers.

Sightless eyes on a muddy bank
Seeing all in their stare,
Result of a childish prank?
Result of one who dared!

Sightless eyes on a muddy bank,
Beaten heart lies so still,
Water laps around its flanks.
Airless lungs did fill.

Sightless eyes on a muddy bank,
Who do I call or tell?
Of this body that has sank,
Lonely as the man that fell?

Ron Nicholas

THE 11TH SEPTEMBER 2001

We all heard the news and wept
We watched in horror and couldn't accept
There is no way we will forgive or pardon
That evil man by the name of bin Laden
He caused so much hurt and so much pain
We have to stop him or he'll do it again
He will be captured whatever the cost
Cos think of those whose lives were lost
People out there wanna settle a score
And now Britain and America fight the war
We will not stop or ever cease
Until we can live in total peace
It's sickening to think what happened at Twin Towers
And all that stands now are condolences and flowers.

Sonia Cusdin

TIME

Time is what you're doing babe and time is what it takes
To repent your sins and pay the price for those terrible mistakes.
Time has no sense of humour - time doesn't think or feel,
It cannot grasp the concept of living behind those bars of steel.
Time isn't just the hands of a clock going round and round,
It's the amount of time we have left to live going down and down.
So spend your time to love and better yourself - for there is no cost,
Then maybe in time you'll be reunited with the love and life you lost.

Dizzy D

AN ODD 'PHANTASY' ODE TO MY PUSSY CAT, PLODDY PLODDERINGS

Ploddy is a little sugar
And he likes playing rugger.
He scored 3 tries for England, once,
Then, disaster, the ball hit him on the bonce.
That was more than Ploddy could take,
So the England team he did forsake.
Off he went to New Zealand to live
And to the All Blacks, his services he did give -
They loved him,
So, he is not coming *back!*

J E Wilson

AT THE HEALTH CLUB

I sit upon this bike a-pedalling quick,
The sun streams in, I wish I were outside
And faster, stronger, work the thighs so thick
For fitness, health and weight loss now I glide;
Like birds above, a-flying so free,
But personal trainer hovers close at hand,
E'er watchful, any slacking off he'll see,
So now to run, the fastest in the land.
Ten minutes seem a hundred, so to me
And now to step and squeeze and pump that iron,
I'll pull those weights, these biceps to improve,
I feel as strong as any female lion
And fat has shifted, which before didn't move!
At last, the longed-for soak I would not miss,
The steam room and jacuzzi - utter bliss!

Verner Hepple

FEELINGS

Feelings of anger,
Feelings of hate,
Feelings are strong
When you have to wait.

You sit there and worry
About what could be,
Are they all staring,
Or is it just me?

You stand up straight
And walk to the door,
Are they all staring
Just like before?

They say you are anxious,
Quite troubled I see,
Feeling so worried,
Even about me.

You get short of breath,
Dizzy sometimes,
I feel I must say,
It's all in your mind.

Feelings of worry,
Feelings so strange,
Must learn to cope
With all of this range.
Feelings of love and passion's desire,
Must learn to cope
And put out the fire.

Daniel Roberts

TWINS

Two babies lying side by side
The scan decides, the mother cries
Tears of joy, of shock, of fright
Years of trying and now delight.

Two babies lying side by side
Skin quite pink, blue eyes so bright
Healthy, happy, born at two
Sisters, but o dear, who is who?

Two toddlers standing side by side
Kate has the doll and Zoe cries
Mum shouts out, 'Come on you two,'
Another battle, but loving too.

Tears of laughter
Tears of joy
Thank goodness they're girls not boys
Hours of cuddles and kisses too
Mum's still tearful but hopeful too.

Jeanette Lloyd

THE CARE HOME

Saddle the day with laughter
Tender words and true,
Yet solitude and silence lie in wait for you.
Supervised sunset, warden-controlled care,
Join the others playing bingo
Never!

Steve Mason

DEEP EMOTIONS

When life seems too much to bear,
You really believe that no one cares.
Hours are spent with a heavy heart,
Oh to put them all in a wheelbarrow cart.

Children you bear are always there
But the love for a man is so hard to share.
Arms wrapped around you, oh so tight,
To spend hours together throughout the night.

It's just like glass the heart is shattered,
To understand what I had done wrong comes later.
Unloved, insecure, confidence slipped,
But for most you hold a tight lip.

How to pick up the pieces, I just can't,
The fight within me is on a declining slant.
I cannot take any more pain and sorrow,
So I shall close me within for no man to borrow.

The next time you hold a woman tight,
Think of her as well as your insight.
The friendship I had with you I shall treasure,
I just pray I can turn this hurt to pleasure.

The moral of this verse is true,
Life is too short to be treated so cruel.
Think the situation out before you dive in,
Because to hurt a woman like this is surely a sin.

W J Martin

LEAVING HOME

You took me under your wing,
I've only had your songs to sing,
I could never compete with you,
So I spread my wings and flew,
Now my heart is broken in two,
The biggest mistake was leaving you.

I have to stand on my own,
There is no going back now,
I know I'll make it somehow,
Sometimes I think of you and home,
I have my own friends, so I'm not alone.

What we had, it's all gone,
It's time for us to move on,
We all change with time,
Please do not worry, I'm fine.

I have my life ahead of me,
The world is one big discovery,
Just think of the wonders I can see,
I will never forget what you've done for me.

I want to thank you so much,
I'm sorry we never kept in touch,
You will always be my best friend,
Right until the very bitter end.

Michael McNulty

THE WEDDING

Nervously waiting, the church is full to the brim
All on the left are here for her, on the right here for him
People looking forward waiting for the wedding march
The groom sits anxious as his throat starts to parch.

The best man checks his pocket for the rings he had to bring
The organist checks the music as the choir wait to sing
The mother of the bride has tears yet to fall
Dad checks final arrangements for the reception at the hall.

The light shines down the aisle as the bride begins to walk
She's looking just as beautiful as everybody thought
Over his shoulder the groom does peer
The best man checks the rings again the time is nearly here.

They meet together at the altar exchanging a loving glance
The groom is full of pride as he steadies up his stance
'Dearly beloved, we are gathered here today . . .'
The opening of the service the reverend has to say.

The service goes so smoothly without a single hitch
The best man stops fidgeting no rings to make him itch
Outside for the photos and confetti in every way
The little things to remember on this a special day.

Geoffrey Graham

SHOPPERS' NIGHTMARE

I've seen you, little trolley,
Just lurking by the door
With your wheels that work
And those that don't,
But drag along the floor.

When I see you coming,
I hold my breath and wait
To see if you go left or right
Or run over my poor 'plates'.

You nip around the corners,
Collide with my poor legs
And without a by your leave,
Go off to meat and veg.

You park in aisles all on your own
Amongst the beans and peas.
Your owner gone, you look forlorn,
No one can pass or leave.

You won't go where you're asked to,
I'm sure you smirk or grin,
When your owner tries to turn to left
And you go right again.

You're taken from the cash point
And parked behind a car,
Whilst all the goods that are therein
Are put in the boot so large.

Your owner goes off on her way,
You're left alone again,
To stand in wind and cold and rain,
It does seem such a shame.

But it serves you right, you trolley,
For all the trouble caused,
With your wheels that work
And those that don't,
Just lurking by the door.

Ken Cufflin

MALLORCA

We flew from Glasgow in the rain
And lightly landed here in Spain
Seeking sea, sand, surf and sun
In a temperature of ninety-one.

To our spacious apartment a random breeze
Brought the fragrance of orange trees
And laughter and voices murmuring low
As lovers splashed in the pool below
While we leaned on the balcony, sipping wine
Completely relaxed and feeling fine.

Then a party started on the second floor
And the night got noisier than before
Loud music pulsed out of the door
Girls were cheering and screaming for more
Sleep became impossible so we listened too
Curious like our neighbours and enjoying the view
We even thought of joining them as the night wore on
For the chances were that no one would be sleeping till dawn.

But security came at 3am, voices raised and torches shone
And after a noisy argument the revellers were gone
With all the excitement over, the spectators vanished soon
And we retired into our beds and lay comatose till noon.

When after a healthy breakfast - cereal, juice and toast
Outfitted in shorts and T-shirts we headed for the coast
Leaving Ca Sabones, strolling down the hill
Into Palma Nova then walking further still
Along the new-tiled promenade with golden sand below
Where bronzed and topless bodies were lying in a row
Making them rather similar in a strange, hypnotic way
To the glinting silver bodies of the fish shoals in the bay.

Stewart Dunlop

PROGRESS

I could not see a future, I really did not care,
I lived just one day at a time, glad just to be here.
I started at the art group, I really did not mind
Where I sat or what I did, not knowing what I'd find.
But oh how pleased I am, I went along and tried,
I now look forward to the art and what I do with pride.
I also joined the journal group and started then to write
It was very difficult at first, I tried with all my might,
But soon my pen flowed freely, as it all came tumbling out,
It sorted out my feelings and what life is all about,
Some sad and poignant verses expressed my point of view;
Giving me a chance to communicate my inner thoughts to you.
Now I'm enthusiastic and the words pour from my pen;
I cannot get them down in time, before I start again.
Another thought, a great idea when it is in my head
But it does not sound quite so good, after it is read!

Shirley Joy Dean

LIFE

Life is one of those things
That everyone learns to accept.
Is sometimes fun and sometimes not
But no one can ever reject.

Not in the beginning at least,
At the start of a whole new existence
When they're a new baby child
Expected to travel the distance

Of what is known as life.
Four score years and ten, it's said
Is how long you have to live.
Some stay more and some less instead.

It's up to you
What you do with it,
Use it or waste
Whatever you see fit.

Life always has a beginning.
The start of a creation.
A wondrous process
Happening in every nation.

First there's a thought,
An idea, a conception
To begin an existence
And hope for a good reception

From those already here,
Who have made a start
On the road of their lives
In which we can all play a part.

Geoff Penycate

SLEEP

My head on pillow, soft I lay,
I close my eyes and drift away
And float into another day,
Departing with a sigh.

Today will be but history,
Tomorrow in the future be
And sleeping twixt them both is me,
As life just slips on by.

In slumber everything is mine
And life is of the finest wine.
In dreams my sun will always shine,
There'll be no cloudy day.

For slumber be a tonic fair,
Sleep with all mankind I share.
On par with tramp or millionaire,
So let me drift away.

Brian L Margetts

A Day Trip To Oxford

If a visit to Oxford is your desire,
These words of advice are what you require.
Buy a detailed map or a really good guide,
If you are arriving by car then use the Park & Ride.

Oxford is 'The city of dreaming spires,'
Where you can count a multitude of bicycle tyres.
A hundred buses on the street,
A thousand summer tourists on their feet.

There are quiet places to be found
In the university parks and the college grounds.
You can take a tour to learn Oxford's history,
Or search out the location of an Inspector Morse mystery.

Go down to the river and take out a punt,
Try not to fall in, or hit the people in front.
Museums to visit, there are quite a few,
Climb the steps of a tower and admire the view.

The old covered market is a place you must see,
They have butchers and bakers with shops to take tea.
It's so full of character, somewhere quite unique,
Walk in off the High Street and have a quick peek.

If you walk into Broad Street along to the end,
Discover the Sheldonian Theatre built by Sir Christopher Wren.
Then just around the corner, down a street named the Turl,
Find the Bodleian Library, one of the oldest in the world.

So many great people have had links with this city,
Prime ministers, scientists, sportsmen and persons literary.
Captains of industry and churchmen, the list just goes on,
From this famous old place with their honours they have won.

There is so much in Oxford to fill up your day,
In the evening perhaps a classical concert or even a play.
If you spend all day walking it can be a strain,
So promise yourself that one day you will come back again!

Steve Cannon

CONTEMPLATION

My happiness does not depend
Upon gain, or he, or she
But on me
And the way in which
I choose to see
In a world of chaos
Trouble and scorn
Hope is in the cry
Of a baby newly born
One of millions
Part of humanity
As a drop of rain
Forms part of the mighty sea
I realise I was meant to be
For without the drops of rain
There would be no sea
And without you or me
No humanity.

P Neild

MIDDLE AGE DREAD

Now a middle-aged man
With a middle-age mind
Finding that nature can be
Quite exceedingly unkind.
The lost mane of hair that flowed in your youth,
Old war stories that date you
As a little long in the tooth,
Sharp eyesight that dims
As cataracts set in,
More opportunities that say out
Instead of welcome in.
Yet fear not the fear of your
Personal setting sun,
Just slow down and walk
You're too old to run.

Don Lambert

KARAOKE KING

I don't care if it's wet or dry,
I'm not fussed about the colour of the sky
Cos all I wanna do is sing,
Just call me The Karaoke King.

When I'm up there on the big, empty stage
Singing the song that is all the rage
I can make the rafters ring
Because I am - The Karaoke King.

It's kinda lonely with no band
Like a single shell on a beach of sand
But I don't need backing girls or boys
Just an audience that makes no noise
And listens to the singer sing
Especially when it's The Karaoke King.

I follow the music everywhere
Will stand on a box or even a chair
With a microphone and guitar of air
I don't give a damn, just don't have a care
All I wanna do is sing
Because I am The Karaoke King.

I can do Presley's moody style
But I don't do Cliff, well not for a while
I can do Robbie, Shaggy and Sting
I can sing almost anything
That's why they call me The Karaoke King.

Jack Couch

DEAD IGNORANT

So many tales of long and old
So many secrets still untold
Who were they to laugh and mock?
They weren't as wise as my grandfather clock.

They were so young and wondering, still
She was always keen to take the pill
But he wouldn't use
And she wouldn't carry

Bang, bang. They're dead.

D S Edwards

GREEN

Olive and lime, bottle and jade,
Every imaginable shade.
Tune the senses, feast the eyes,
Revel in the surprise.
Green rampantness prevails
Throughout the dales,
The cliff tops and the hills.
Lush luxuriance fills
The garden hedgerow,
And the nooks where the wild flowers grow.
And burgeoning full,
The vegetable
Patch portends
Its veritable dividends.
So much so,
That I will never know
Or understand
The demand
For beans and peas of equal size,
Or the desire to artificially fertilise.

Ruth Sharville

THE DIET

I open my wardrobe and yes, it's still there,
The small size ten that I will never wear.
I always hope that I will lose some weight,
But I do like my food and my will power is not great.
At lunch time I think I will have just once slice,
When it is gone I think yes, that was very nice.
I try to say no when the cakes come along,
I know I'll have another, even though it's wrong.
I cut all the fat off my meat before dinner,
If only I stop eating it, I'm sure I would be thinner.
I did try aerobics but could not keep time,
But what did you expect? I am sixty-nine.
My husband loves me just as I am,
But I will lose weight if I possibly can.
I really don't like being this size,
It would make me so happy to win that prize.

R M Wilcox

DYING FOR LIFE

Two little stars that shine so bright
Out of reach, but not of sight
Beautiful beyond compare
To blight your sparkle, so unfair
The world is yours, but not so mine
I love you enough to let you shine.
Sprinkle your magic in far array
Make your mark on the world, live for today.
My star stopped shining long ago
Its tainted surface began to show
And all the other stars around
One by one fell earthward bound.
Except you two that shine so bright
Your sparkle threatened by my tainted blight
I will not let your stars dull and die
To fall infected from the sky
I love you so much, I want you to shine
And to save your stars, I must extinguish mine.

Suzanne Adams

PAIN

I only wanted to be normal,
I only wanted to be loved,
But the pain it just took over,
It travelled in my blood.

The anger boiled over,
It swirled through my veins
And there right from that moment
I would never be the same.

The pain got to the heart of me
And turned my world around,
I couldn't make a movement,
Could barely make a sound.

When I couldn't take any more
And thought my life was at its end,
I was given the strength to carry on
And turned pain into my friend.

And there you are every day
Trying to gain back control,
But I will never let you back in,
For I have courage within my soul.

Sharon Simpson

CUPID'S CLOUD

Flood warnings are issued with effect from today,
For unusual weather is heading your way.
Showers of kisses and cuddles and love
Will fall in torrents from the heavens above
And this love will 'reign' for all of time
If you will be my Valentine.

Sean Coll

QUESTIONS

I saw his ghost - no face or limb
With arms outstretched I welcomed him
He glided, stopped and looked at me
He'd gone - my mind as spaced as he.

I welcomed his return next day
So much I'd wanted him to say
The questions came from me as well
Had he reached Heaven and bypassed Hell?

What was life like in land beyond
Were loved ones waiting there to bond
Was it worth the wait to seek one's rest
To reap reward for life caressed?

He didn't visit me again
The experts said, 'A soul in pain'
No answers came, for he'd just stared
I like to think that he'd just cared.

Eileen E Overton

GREAT WORKS

In 1642 the mathematician Galileo died,
the same year that a young boy arrived.
He studied at Cambridge and never vague,
returning home during the great plague.

Through his prism he did split white light,
seeing red, green and blue was a new sight.
These he found are the light primary colours,
and by mixing them up you can make any others.

He's now well known as Sir Isaac Newton,
who sat in his garden with his suit on.
His favourite spot was beneath a tree,
he used to sit there quite frequently.

One day it seemed the apples were red,
as he was relaxing one fell on his head.
Straight away he thought and had a quirk,
he rushed to his room to study and work.

Studying hard with lots of investigation,
he came up with his theory of gravitation.
The universe was then regulated by gravity,
till Einstein put forward about relativity.

P J Davies

SOD'S LAW

I walk down the street and what do I see?
Someone on a bike coming straight at me.
Does he go in the road? No, not he.

I wait for a bus then four in a row
Are heading this way, but for me? Oh no.
My bus is the one on a go-slow.

Saturday post office what a nightmare,
The only day workers have time to spare
So why that day OAPs are there?

I make a phone call, my TV won't work
Talking to people this company shirk,
I press the wrong button - what a berk.

Shopping at the shortest queue I can
All queues move but I'm still where I began
I wait like the invisible man.

Lottery next, my numbers are jumping
Here they come and my heart is thumping
Now in the bin, my tickets I'm dumping.

This is sod's law in its rawest form
The way of life one must conform
For me, anyway, this is the norm!

Irene Carroll

ANGER

You took my life away,
how could you dare?
I screamed and I shouted,
you did not care,
I felt the anger deep within,
you threw me away,
in life's dustbin.
I think I feel the teardrops flow,
so how could you leave, why did you go?
Because you're a man,
what do you care, that's why I'm angry,
life's just not fair.

Pauline Jones

I AM GRATEFUL FOR THIS DAY

Plants and pots and dirty hands,
Flowers, weeds and gardening plans.
Delight in checking every night
A bud that opens by moonlight.

Reaping vegetables, picking flowers,
Thinking little of the hours,
Caring hands tend the seeds
Giving water, pulling weeds.

Gardening gives a special time
To exercise, or rest the mind,
To think of something or of naught,
Of what you know, or what you've thought.
To take a mental pause . . . and say,
'I am grateful for this day.'

Mary Beck

SOMERSET

The rolling hills of Somerset, ancient and green
Mysterious Isle of Avalon, snuggled between
Mendip and Polden, with a view to the sea,
       Calling, calling, calling to me.

The Quantock hills where heather and whortleberries grow
Where the deer can run freely, both red deer and roe
These too have a view looking out to the sea
       Calling, calling, calling to me.

The Blackdowns, ah the Blackdowns, mysterious and old
Strange things used to happen there I have been told
Old tales that will not die, no smoke without fire
       Calling, calling, no I'll retire.

Three Michael hills rising up from the moor
Brent Knoll, Burrow Mump, then of course the Tor
Ancient legends as old as Father Time
Deep, dark, brooding peat bogs, criss-crossed by rhyne
       Calling, calling, calling through time.

Mysterious, dank, damp caverns, once home to men
The hunters and gatherers reigned supremely then
Stalagmite met stalactite, where once dwelt a witch
Where runs an ice-cold river, waters dark as pitch
       Calling, calling, heritage rich.

Men lived in huts built up clear of water
Goods were the dowry when marrying a daughter
This then is Summerland, where islands used to be
Lapped and surrounded on all sides my the sea
       Calling, calling, calling to me.

Dora Watkins

REFLECTION ON OLD AGE

I look in the mirror and what do I see?
I can't believe it - is that me?
Baggy eyes and a crumpled face,
A travesty of the human race!
Lines, the envy of British Rail!
When did it all begin to fail?

Never a beauty - I just got by,
Look at me now! Mirrors don't lie,
Scraggy neck and wrinkled skin
And how did I get that extra chin?
Everything seems to drop and sag,
Is this me, or some old hag?

Memories begin to fade,
Where did I put that hearing aid?
I go to the kitchen, open a drawer,
What on earth am I looking for?
I know I'm really young at heart,
Why do I seem to be falling apart?

Web sites, chat rooms, surf the net,
E-mail, dot com! Heavens, what next?
A foreign language I can't take,
Once 'speed' meant racing, 'crack' meant break,
'Gay' meant happy, 'queer' meant strange,
Why does everything have to change?

Five-foot-six I used to be,
Now I'm only five-foot-three,
My brains say, 'Try to stand up straight,'
My bones will not co-operate!
So here I am, by age diminished,
Life was good once - is this finished?

H Leventhall

LIFE

Love the life you live,
live the life you love.
As you take each breath, each day,
remember it's a gift from above.

I, you, them,
we all have a part in this life.
Look much deeper than the exterior
and surely there will be less strife.

Free to be who we want to be,
as the bird that flies in the sky.
Make sure you endeavour to fulfil your dreams
or life will pass you by.

Evolving into a better being
is what we should all reach for,
when you live your life to the full,
you cannot ask for more.

Maizetta Trotman

LIGHT AS A FEATHER, QUIETER THAN A MOUSE

Magical starships, flight-path to Earth
Crystalline fuselage, mystical birth,
Every one different yet all seem identical,
Blanket the landscape in silence, intangible.

Heavy the boughs that cry in the trees,
Bearing the weight of the icy-cold breeze
That carried its craft to their bare limbs,
Where shivering, shaking and quaking so grim.

Rustling gently the wind tosses her head
And strikes cold, poor robin, so radiant red
Against pure white snow jewels crowning all with glory
Your curtain on the woods today was a real life fairy story.

E L Tanton

A PHOTOGRAPH

A photograph is a memory,
One to treasure through the years,
One to keep beside you
Through happiness and tears.

A photograph is a keepsake
From which you'll never part,
A photograph has a special place
To keep beside your heart.

A photograph to look at
When one is feeling blue,
To smile and say, I love you,
A photograph of you.

Jacqueline Marriott

WHY?

A wondrous sunset o'er mountain and sea
A world full of beauty for you and for me
The smile of a child, the courage of men
Love and devotion existing, but then
Why do we let demons of jealousy and greed
Creep into our hearts to destroy this dream?
To permeate our family, country as well
And corrupt making followers act suicidal
While governments retaliate to acts of terror
Till war becomes imminent and peace a mere whisper?
Why let these demons repeat history and plan
A war to end wars, destroy every last man?
Let all thinking clearly resolve to defeat
By joining together their task to complete
The final removal from all thought and deed
Of violent jealousy and evil greed
For in war the sad truth will always remain
While the guilty escape, the innocent are slain
Then may leaders of countries cause enmities to cease
Giving future generations the right to have peace
Only then will our children inherit our dream
Of a heaven on earth filled with love in each scene.

R M Green

SCIENCE KING

Conflicting views
Are so confused,
All I love might be destroyed.
Life we lose
For what we use,
This sacrilege has me annoyed.

Lungs of the earth,
What is oxygen worth?
Radiant rainforest, chop her down,
Pollute our air,
Devoid of care,
Change the climate so we drown.

May be war
We stand before,
With all the weapons we devise,
Of peril proud
Kill the crowd,
Contamination fill the skies.

Oh, science king,
Extinction bring,
Did your creation come with shield,
Where will you hide
When all has died,
When you have poisoned every field?

Oh cry, mankind,
For clever mind
Is cutting callous at your throat.
Can it be sane
This brilliant brain,
That death and disaster does provoke?

Becky Hardiman

MUDDLED MEMORIES

Another dreary day;
Grey clouds fill the sky.
Rain pelts down,
For shelter birds must fly.
Matching muddled memories
Meandering in my mind.

Children always squabbling
And screaming at each other.
Fighting over stupid things;
Who'd want to be a mother?
Matching muddled memories
Meandering in my mind.

Surrounded by well-meaning people
Talking at me, why not to me?
Only those who really understand
Know best to let me be.
Matching muddled memories
Meandering in my mind.

The one who's always by my side
And endures me day to day,
Is patient, caring and kind
And knows the words to say.
Matching muddled memories
Meandering in my mind.

The sky turns blue, out creeps the sun;
I'm no longer crying.
Now it seems, behind the clouds
I've found my silver lining.
My mind is clear, no more confused
And muddled memories no longer matter.

Samantha Gribble

HERON

Hunched heron, dignified and grey,
Sunshine warming your back while the fish gently play,
Your movement is graceful and without sound,
Hunched heron, you hold me starbound.
Tall and graceful and happy in solitude,
Waiting for insects and any other fine food,
Aware of movement and things that stray near,
Hunched heron, a prince amongst birds, that holds you so dear.
You hold yourself regal without rush or sound,
Crest on head, your crown.

L Terry

THE HEART

The mind is full of doubts
Nowhere to turn
Oh, how the pain does burn
Pretending to be asleep in bed
No one would believe the tears you shed

Where is your life going, you don't belong
Your lonely heart no longer sings a love song
Your youth has passed you like a cloud
And you didn't make a fuss or a sound
You can't help being the naive person that you are
But, the angels switched on the light and now you see a star

Oh, what a feeling of joy and elation
Please come share this magical sensation
You are now free to read a book when you please
And listen to the radio without being teased
No longer wasting away
Now you can have your say

Your mind is finally clear
And you weren't that paranoid dear
Your suspicions were not in your mind
Even though you appeared to be blind

You're always the last to know
Because we all just go with the flow
You shouldn't mess with someone's heart
It's certain that one day you will feel the dart

Free as the bird that flies high
Now, I'm announcing my goodbye.

Kim Taplin

COME THE REBELATION

The world is surely coming to an end,
Bad manners seem to be a growing trend;
But I'm comforted by this fact -
Polite 'rebels' make a bigger impact . . .

David Hughes

SHOPPING

I'm not a high street shopper
I find it such a bore
All that thumping music
In every single store

I'm not a bargain hunter
Two for the price of one
No! Put me in the country
Where I am free to run

I don't want to battle through
A hundred thousand faces
Put me in the countryside
In the open spaces

The thought of facing shopping malls
Fills me with a shiver
Let me walk in forests
Or down by the river

And as for January sales
Those bargains, just a farce
I'm not a high street shopper
Shopping no! I'll pass.

Esmond Hannon

WARMONGER'S POEM

Let's start World War Three.
Drop bombs on a foreign country.
Our planes will haunt the sky,
While innocent women and children die.

Time to show the UN our moral autonomy,
So we'll pay the blood price for democracy.
Our armed forces will sweat and toil,
In order for capitalists to possess the oil.

We could pretend to really want peace,
Hoping the plight of the refugees will cease,
But our real problem is the global economy,
We'll murder and kill in the name of humanity.

This is a warning to any rogue state,
We'll take you on with all our hate.
Crocodile tears for collateral damage.
We only think *their* governments are savage.

It is the beginning of a new arms race,
To protect us all from the terror we face.
Civilians dread the horror of a nuclear eruption,
So we'll find those weapons of mass destruction.

A good conflict would be so much fun,
Another chance to say our values have won.
Have we learnt the lessons of world history?
Whatever, anyway - who cares about apathy?

Julius Howard

THE THOUGHTS OF A GREAT GRANDMOTHER

Now I'm in my twilight years
I ponder on my joys and fears,
Of when I was young and there was a war,
When family and neighbours were our very core.

We had very little and treasured what we had,
Though it meant growing up without my dad,
He was a sailor fighting to free
The right to live for you and me.

I wouldn't change places with the youth of today,
Too much, too soon has come their way,
Their lives being spoilt by modern day stress
And I ask myself, is this really progress?

The shootings and stabbings of war on the streets,
Never knowing what horrors we are going to meet,
Our lives are decreed by drugs, drink and greed,
So is this what was fought for when we were freed?

For a better life the solution is plain,
Like driving a car, get in the right lane.
By kindness and love and grateful for life,
Be carefree and happy and free of all strife.

Joy Hanlon

THE FINAL CALL

Hello, Dad,
How are you today?
So many things you'd like to say.
I hear your voice and get your drift,
As through your many thoughts you sift.

Those bees, your passion and your dream,
The never-ending ways they seem
That when you always come to find
They never cease to amaze the workings of your mind.

As time begins to flow
And you begin to slow,
Little did I know that this
Would be the final flare
As at the closing point I hear
You say, 'Take care!'

Sheila Lewis

DUGUID AND MASON

So much fear I have to hide
Dearly loved and nearly died
All this pain I tried to mask
How I wish I could have cried

Smiling faces where I look
Caring hearts where they touch
Hide their pains I can see
Still they care just for me

As I sleep I know they're there
Watching me with all their care
As I dream through the night
I hold on tight with all my might

Now that morn it has come
Soon I know I will be done
Now I pray I rid this curse
How can I say, thank you nurse?

Jason Greenshields

UNTITLED

I say to my grandma on this very sad day
That you will be missed in every such way,
You were very loving and very kind,
Someone like you is just so hard to find.
A heart of gold, so pure, so true,
It came so natural, that was just you.
Always there to lend a hand
Or to sit and listen and understand.
To make us smile, if you were down,
To brighten our day all around.
Dear Grandma, you will be sadly missed,
All memories of you will always exist.
You will always be there
In our thoughts and our minds,
Always there till the end of time.
All loved ones stand here today
And remember you, as we pray
All your suffering has been released,
God bless you, Grandma,
Rest in peace.

Claire Williams

WHAT ARE YOU?

Are you real or in my head?
Are you alive or are you dead?
Are you able to breathe fresh air?
Hello, where are you, are you there?
Speak to me if you can,
Are you ghost or are you man?
Can you see the sun in the sky,
Or do you sit on the clouds and cry?
If you're a ghost, do you have feelings
And do you have thoughts that have no meanings?
What can you say or can you speak
Or is it through humans that you seek?
What are the things that you really miss,
Do you seek love or happiness?
Do you wish that you were alive,
Or is it better being dead so you can hide?

Marie Harper

TO MY UNKNOWN FATHER - CEDRIC DOVER

Those twinkling eyes,
That handsome face
And from what I've learned,
He had such grace.

Such a clever man
To write as he did,
Why didn't I know him
When I was a kid?

Didn't he love me?
I'll never know,
Unanswered questions
Upset me so.

I might have been happy
If he had been there,
There was much to be given,
So much to share.

Most adults look back
On their happy years.
All of my memories
Fill me with tears.

Valerie Robertson

THE TAPE RAN OUT

I tried and I tried but it didn't want to come
I'm in a dark hole now and it's cold and I feel numb.
I look to the open sky but I can't get any light
The walls are closing in and I begin to lose the fight.

My lightweight body is holding up and battling on,
But in my mind the war is over and the struggle has gone.
I lie on my own halfway there, only expecting the end
And I want the pain to stop, but for this I have to pretend.

Unbearable torture has taken a sweet likening to me
So it better be worth it, Jesus better invite me in for tea.
I guess the end is nearing, but now I am blind
Why is this necessary, I beg you, can't you be more kind?

Don't turn your back, I'm talking to you, to God almighty
He's now answered my call and He holds me tightly.
I'm not bitter, it's for the best, that I have no doubt.
I'm only history because the tape ran out!

Cameron McAulay

A WEDDING SPEECH

Now I am standing up here with not much to say
Because I know you have all heard it before
So I will read you what I have written on this paper
That way it won't be too much of a bore

Now I would like to thank you all for coming
To a wedding that was held on this day
It went off rather well as far as I can tell
And all those who were involved had their say

Now the bride looked divine and the bridegroom was fine
And the bridesmaids were all dressed the same
They looked rather nice it was a good choice
And I hope you are all glad that you came

Now I would like to welcome Geoff into this family
And the rest of the family as well
So let's all be friends on this joyous occasion
But what the future may bring, who can tell?

Now my daughter and Geoff are well suited
I trust him, I haven't a care
He will look after my daughter, he will do what he can
And that's my opinion that's fair

Now the caterers have been, they have done a good job
The tables look well-laden and neat
It looks just like Heaven, I will be glad when it's half-seven
And we can all get something to eat

Now my speech has ended, it's time to relax
And shake off the doom and gloom
So raise up your glass and give a big cheer
And we will toast the bride and groom.

John Allen Pinches

LOVE

I do not know what to do
For I think it's
Happening to me and you.
The feeling goes deep down inside,
For I wish I
Could just run and hide,
Far away from prying eyes,
Somewhere in a different time.
Left alone, I'll be fine.

Brendan J Meadows

UNCONDITIONAL LOVE

She greets me every morning
And she's with me every day.

She scratches and she growls,
Sending strangers on their way.

She loves to have her tummy rubbed,
Long walks along the shore,
Her squeaky toys her special treats,
Her blanket on the floor.

Who is this 'she' I write about,
Who gives unconditional love?

She is my pal, my trusted friend,
She is of course, my dog.

Barbara Stone

VAGABOND

A vagabond am I who takes of life's sweet pleasures,
A vagabond am I who has in life no measures.
I take of life what comes and don't cry for tomorrow,
There is no reason why; endure life's joys and sorrows.
Take each and every day is if there is no more,
Sweet gift of life I share, to worship and adore.
I stroll along God's land take in his gift of beauty;
I have no sense of loyalty, endurance, work or duty.
Move on from place to place, I leave my friends behind me,
Such as in life itself, no guaranteed stability.
Life is for us to take, to share each joy and pleasure,
A vagabond am I without such rules or measure.
I wander here and there from one place to another;
I have no brother, sister, cousin, child or mother.
I know not where I go nor where I'm travelling from,
Sweet freedom is for me, I travel round and roam.
Sweet wine of life I sip, wherever that may be,
Meander down the road, alone I am set free.
A vagabond am I who takes of life's sweet pleasures,
A vagabond am I who has in life no measures.

Wendy Evans

SORROW

I'm sorry I hurt you, so sorry I lied,
I'm sorry you cried when your nan died.
I'm sorry I destroyed you when I pushed you away,
I'm sorry I never saw the pain inside.
I'm sorry I found a place to hide.
I'm sorry things turned so sour,
I thought our love had a greater power.
Alas it was not meant to be,
So I'll be sorry for eternity.

K Dellow

A GAME OF CHOICE

What is this game we play? The hectic chase? The race we run?
Where's the prize? What do you hope to have won?
Is it a face you see from afar,
That knowing glance that says who you are?
That instant connection, that vital spark
That burning light that breaks through the dark?

Could it be a jewel you dig from a mine,
Give a little effort and you know it will shine?
Is it the spark or is it the jewel?
In the game either can rule.
In this life we are all dealt cards,
21 wins, hit 22 and you could get scared.

You have an investment in one that's going to pay
The other gives you feelings no one can take away
Cost of the jewel is in time,
The other is finding what you may never find
The jewel and the spark, the spark and the jewel
Both can be right, both can be cruel.

Who knows which road to pick?
Choose the route you best fit.
So I say this, listen to the birds sing
And choose the one that makes you happy without doing a thing.

Allen Hunt

A SMILE

A smile is something special
Which all of us can share
It doesn't cost a penny
Just shows we really care.

A smile can break down barriers
And make us many friends
And if we've had a quarrel
It helps to make amends.

So make somebody happy
Please wear a smile each day
And all life's joys and blessings
Will surely come your way.

Deirdre Atherton

JUST ANOTHER VICTIM OF THE AMBIENT MORALITY

Do you even see me as you walk by
Is it because I'm so low and you're so high
Could you look into my eyes, just for a while
Do I seem so bad to you, am I so vile.

And if I asked you for some help, what would you say
Would you even give a little, or would you just turn away
Though your pockets are deep, and you can afford
To spare a few coins for those who are ignored.

And if you glanced down, what would you see
You'd see a hand, a hand that needs.
Would you take that hand, or give me a sign
That I share your world, and you share mine.

It isn't my fault that I'm down here
Would you still feel no pity if I shed a tear
So don't turn your back, just like the rest
Because I'm not the worst, and you're not the best.

But you walk away, back to your life
Back to your warm house, and your loving wife.
Leaving me huddled here, hungry and alone
Crying because I don't have a home of my own.

Carl Gravestock

BATHROOM BLUES

When you washed your hands and face
Was the towel hung in its place?
Was the toothbrush in the rack?
I wonder just who put it back!

On the toilet . . . business done
Was there paper for your bum?

When you took a bath last night
Was the bath all shiny bright?
Oh good it was!
I wonder who keeps cleaning tidemarks off for you?

When you stepped out of the tub
Did you want a nice, warm rub?
With a nice warm towel you found (on the rail)
Not on the ground!

Funny how things seem to be
Replaced for you . . . but not for *me!*
I fumble for the damp, wet towel
Guess what? It's nowhere near the rail
It's on the floor, behind the door!

And toilet paper
There's no more
And as a mum
I *seethe* and say
Who used the last *bit* anyway?

Wendy Wootton

RAINY DOORWAY

Another day
Without much pay
People rushing past.
I sit here in a doorway,
Another day to dream.
How mean -
No end to this routine.
Day in, day out
Until I discover the meaning
Of happy smiles and people's feelings.
Dry clothes, a bed, a home.
How can I hang on -
When did it all go wrong?
One pound thrown down to my cap
On the ground.
The dog is grateful
Tail wagging, always hopeful.
I love that tail
But I feel frail.
Another few hours and it's time for tea,
What will it be?
Another pound hits the ground.
I'm lucky today,
Even though the sky is grey.
My friend and I in the rainy doorway.

Carole Palmer

THE GARDEN VILLAGE FAYRE

This is a dream of some ladies rare
who went to the Garden Village Fayre
dressed with splendour in their gowns
as if they were on Epsom Downs.

Pamela Pansy wore beads and bangles
Rosie Rose in pink and sandals
at their best they shuffled by
as Margot Marigold caught their eye.

The sun came out, the Fayre began
when Lady Lupin waved her fan
in radiant blue she looked a treat
and said you may commence to eat.

Sally Snowdrop in her ice-cool bonnet
cut the cake with cream upon it
whilst Dilys Daisy in a yellow dress
said she preferred the egg and cress

Tania Tulip won first prize
for her figure and her size
Patsy Pompom then popped up
and presented Tania with the cup.

The stalls are bare, the day is done
the ladies did enjoy the fun
it's time for bed, the petals close
until the next dream, 'Who knows!'

Fredrick Allan

THE SURPRISE

We're going to a shop today, at least I think that's what it is.
Mommy says it's a surprise for me, but Daddy says it's his.
He tells me then he's joking, as we drive there in the car,
The surprise is for the family; I hope we don't go far.
I start to get excited, as we park outside a wall,
And walk towards a great, big gate then into a little hall.
The receptionist says, 'Come with me, I'll show you all around.'
She opens up another door and says, 'Look what we've found!'
The excitement takes me to a peak, I can't believe my eyes.
Rows and rows of puppy dogs, what a great surprise.
My mom and dad they tell me, that I can take my pick,
Of a puppy dog to take home, so I'd better choose it quick.
I glance into the cages, and straight away I see.
A beautiful pair of big, brown eyes, looking straight at me.
'That one Mom!' I shout aloud, 'That's the one for me.'
I pick him up and cuddle him, a new member of our family.

Richard Ward

CLICHÉ

Silence is golden?
Only when it's loud,
When we are alone, we pine for human sound.

Patience is a virtue?
When we're the one who's waiting
Placed on the other side, patience is forsaken.

At the end of the day?
So which day is that?
The one that defines all reason?
Or turns fiction into fact?

It's better to have loved and lost than to never have loved at all?
It's better to have won the lottery than perpetually being poor.

Home is where the heart is?
Well mine is in my chest,
I suppose Mr Magpie keeps his in his nest!

Life begins at 40?
Or so they say.
39 years are wasted, waiting for that day.

It's the little things that matter?
Well, why live in a house?
Buy a garden shed, replace the dog with a mouse!

You're as old as you feel?
Well I feel 92.
But I haven't got any wrinkles and I don't eat processed stew.

Those were the days?
What, the ones in the past?
If they were so great, why didn't they last?

The beauty of the cliché is that it makes sense.
A phrase with little meaning.
Great! I'm sitting on the fence!

Darren W Simon

ANOTHER WORLD

The air was still, the ground was white
The world stood still that starry night
All around the snow lay deep
Not a sound and not a peep
I stood as still as I could be
And wondered how on earth could he
Make this Earth, beautiful and bright
As it was, that starry night

Then all of a sudden there was quite a flurry
As an owl flew by, in a dreadful hurry
Soaring, soaring very high
Reaching up into the sky
I wonder where he had been that night
As he flew by, just out of sight
The world again stood still that night

Then out of the corner of my eye
A little mouse went scurrying by
Running as hard as he dare try
That wise old owl had passed him by
And once again the world was still
High upon that snowy hill

And just over there, was a snowy white hare
Sitting, nose twitching, giving me a stare
Waiting for the slightest sound
And off he'll go with a leap and bound
So once again on that silent night
The snow came down
On that world so white.

Jean Hughes

EUROPE

With China cup in shaking hand,
Sturdy stick to give him aid.
He slowly wends the garden path
To table seat in leafy shade.
White straw hat covers thinning hair,
Sips the tea near tumbling stream.
Over the wall echoes ball on bat,
With appeals of the village team.
Old church clock strikes evening hour
Fading sun lights a crimson sky.
This old veteran of El-Alamein,
Will he ask the reason why -
Past comrades fell on history's blade
To halt demands a European made?

Bruce Hempsall

CHANGES

Changes, they happen
And some you control,
Others creep up.
You just don't know
How this life's pathway
Will take you along.
Travelling routes
And hoping no wrong
Will come of decisions
That you choose to make.
Maybe pride and dignity
You must forsake,
To embrace this life
And achieve full potential,
To be true to yourself
Is a real essential.

Sue Umanski

WONDER

Have you ever wondered
        What it's like to fly
Midst rolling clouds
        Soft as a sigh?

Or ever pondered
        What it's like to swim
Midst myriad fishes
        Just on a whim?

Or ever thought
        Sat 'round the hearth
What a glorious gift
        This life on Earth?

Just for a moment
        Take time to reflect
On all of the presents
        For you to collect

For *now* is all
        The time at hand
So waste it not
        You understand?

Rhona Gibson

ANCIENT BEHAVIOUR

There he sits in his window, blue rheumy eyes wide,
Watching out for my welfare, like a father, with pride;
Waiting daily for callings, just some time given free,
Sailing notions of hope over pale waves of tea.
He's a mask steeped in hist'ry . . . and myst'ry still yet,
Ever telling me stories, born of England's stiff debt;
And as hands, big and cumbersome, touch my own, frail,
Young and old breach the seasons of sorrow and hale.
How we each feed the other - fun and comfort, and more . . .
All those lessons learned only through friendship's best door.
As he stands - a true gentlemen, legs losing way,
There his balance knocks living right out of his play.
Breathing seems such an effort, for his wheeze fills my heart
With that tad of commotion, thoughts of loss seems to start;
And as nature's safe bet turns its bitterest wheel,
It's his worn out old sofa, that softens God's deal.
Never more will those curtains twitch, nor will they smile,
Now he'll never be reached with that push-buttoned dial.
I can feel him still watching, feel his infinite care,
But at last he's at peace, caught in love's humble prayer.

Angela E Crosbie

WINTERTIME

The alarm is ringing, I open my eyes
Turn off the noise and look up to the skies
It's cold, it's dark and bleak again
How could a place have so much rain
I wake my son for a day at school
He can't be late, it would break a rule
Washed and dressed, without a fuss
He sets off to catch the old school bus
How far away, the summer seems
Not to worry, we have our dreams
Blue skies, sunshine and butterflies flying
Cut the grass whilst the washing is drying
I come down to earth as the wind gets stronger
The winter months seem longer and longer
It's 4 o'clock and the front door opens
School over, down with the books and ball-point pens
Casserole in the oven and coffee in the pot
We look forward to the days when it's nice and hot
It's dark again, so very soon
The only light shines down from the moon
I wonder what tomorrow will bring
Oh well, time to dream of that summer feeling.

Susan Moffatt

FRIENDSHIP

You care for your friends,
And they care for you too.
When you are down, they help you
And when they are down, you help them too.

Friendship is strong when you've got a nice friend;
And when you've got a nice friend to talk to,
You will never be parted.
You will be friends for as long as you live.

Friendship is a great thing to have,
When you're with the right person.
Friends should be there for one another,
And never be apart, never, never!

Laura-Jane Holloran

UNWANTED GUEST

A poltergeist (and it's well known)
Is far from paranormal
You'll never *see* one, but its visits
Are a touch informal
It lives with you for nothing
Manages on thin air
Never eats and never sleeps
But you always know it's there
It moves the furniture around
So it can put its feet up
And if you want a coffee
It throws you out a cup
Floorboards squeak, the carpet's rucked
Noise comes from underground
But you can't quite locate its source,
As no one is around

Exorcism just won't work - they live in churches too
But if you have one in your house
I hope that God's with you -
If you try to get it moved
There is this legal restriction:
There's not a form on which to serve
Your Notice of Eviction . . .

David Thomsett Palmer

MAKING UP

It is 24 hours since I heard your dear voice
And yet I am glowing still
And I know those emotions I felt as we spoke
Were contained by an effort of will.

For you never can know just how marvellous it was
To hear your sweet voice on the line
And I knew as you spoke, by the lilt and the tone,
That all would be well, given time.

I was frightened beforehand, thinking I suppose
That it might not be quite right to call
But I need not have worried
For hearing your pleasant surprise made it right after all.

I have loved you so much and for so long, my dear friend
It has always seemed natural as breathing
But I think that I never loved you quite so much
As on hearing your bright voice, last evening.

Sandra Holmes

INSPIRATION

Re-light that candle, re-start that fire,
Fulfil your passion and live to inspire.
Follow your heart and do as you may,
Fight every challenge that walks your way.
Look out on the world, show off your pride,
Create a new path, with every new stride.
Prepare for the future and remember the past,
Live full the present that only moments shall last.
Hold tight a loved one, befriend an old enemy,
For as fate may play it, it could change your destiny.
Let out your desires, give birth to a new dream,
It can be easier than all what may seem.
Prove right what is wrong, prove false to be true,
Show the world there is none other like you!
Then perhaps you can thank your reason for change,
As it extinguished the obsession you once had for revenge.

Tahira Asghar

A TIME FOR CHANGE

World reports,
World news,
The world's in a mess,
It gives me the blues.

Crime and fighting,
Fighting crime,
Terror and evil,
It's all the time.

War here,
War there,
TV coverage,
Does nobody care?

Rapists and guns,
Knives and theft,
It makes me wonder,
What there is left!

Peace and harmony,
Is what we should give,
So the next generations,
Can peacefully live.

Caroline Hartley

PLEASE FEED THE BIRDS IN WINTER

When Jack Frost bites and days are short
Please try and give a little thought
To every bird who sings its song.
Each summer day, all day long,
It's hard for them to keep well fed
For us it's easy, snug in our bed.
But when water's frozen, where do they drink?
For us our tap is in the sink!
Maybe some nuts or bits of fat
I know they'll really enjoy that
The pleasure that the birds do bring
Make it worthwhile when they sing
Their songs of joy of things so good,
So spare a thought - I think you should.

Barbara Church

PROGRESS

The twentieth century's been and gone
We're well into another one
And as the months come round again
Will they bring happiness or pain?
The brains with which some men are blest
Should be used only for the best
They really should be used to find
Some benefit for mankind
To find a cure for our ills
Whether with treatment or with pills.
A cure for cancer would be fine
Before the year, two ninety-nine
Arthritis should be overcome
And that would mean relief for some
Stop making bombs to maim or kill
And set to making with a will
New drugs or better kinds of food
And thus improve the world for good

Lois Winifred Foster

WASH DAY BLUES

Sorted the whites from the coloureds
And stuffed them in the machine
Two tablets in a bag, this will get my clothes clean
40 degrees it says, for a wash beyond compare
Pressed the appropriate buttons and went off to wash my hair
Twenty minutes later, I walked into the utility
I thought the Amazon River had been diverted into our vicinity
The dog floated down the passage and out of the front door
Why when you want a plumber, the phone they do ignore?
If I had some tools I'd build myself a raft
The neighbours would all say she's finally gone daft
But who will do the ironing and put the clothes away?
Damn I will be a heroine and stay another day.

Eunice Wilson

THROUGH THE EYES OF A CHILD WITH AUTISM

Life through the eyes of an autistic child,
Whatever can it be?
The bullying, harassment, torture and pain
Is very hard to see.

I aim to show what life is like,
Through those soft, tender eyes
So persons no longer torment and despise.

I arose again today, like yesterday,
To another day of living anguish.
The school, the gates of misery,
Where I am subject to pay
Pay the price for being autistic,
Like others have in history.

I cannot understand sarcasm,
These simple words cause offence
And make my empty eyes
The flowing water of incompetence.

In many ways, I'm worse off
Than the blind, the deaf, the lame.
Their problems can be perceived,
But mine are not so plain.

Many people say I'm stupid,
Or simply bad behaved,
For they cannot see my problems
And do not come to my aid.

Alun Evans

STAR ROAD

The mystery of the Great Star Road
Wondrous though it be
Only happens just the once
Throughout eternity
High above the road it weaves
Between the stars it wanders
Destiny is what it leaves
Transporting still vast numbers
Numerous spirits cast by fate
Lost in the storm of time
Always more that will never wait
On their journey to this shrine
The sun, the moon, the planets high
The things we take for granted
Could make up the reason why
Life goes when it is wanted
Death like birth is but a giving
Minuendous beyond all reason
A privilege only for the living
A peaceful alleviation.

Iain Mackenzie

THE ENEMY WITHIN

He stands there, back against the wall.
Fear filling his eyes,
He wants to call out but what's the point?
No one will hear his cries.

Someone should protect him,
Save him from this hell.
No one comes to his rescue
If they would, his soul, he'd sell.

If only he could move his legs,
Then he could run away,
Raw fear paralysed him
Against the wall he has to stay.

Eye to eye with his enemy,
Should he be the first to attack?
They both step towards each other,
Then they both take the same step back.

There's no answer to his dilemma,
He'll be there for the rest of his life.
Then the sound of a key turning in the lock,
Made him pray. Let this be the wife!

His prayers were answered, his wife walked in,
The spider scurried away,
He tried to look cool, but just looks a fool,
His phobia, he lives with every day.

Pamela Pearson

PANIC

Why do I feel this way?
Why do I hurt every day?
Feeling scared, lonely, deep inside.
Is there no one in whom I can confide?

I want to express my fears,
Instead I lay alone in tears.
Panic surrounds me, I have no control,
The pain I feel, deep in my soul.

I feel the pounding of my heart,
Then the dizziness and sickness start.
All I can see is black and white,
Totally lost my hearing and sight.

Hot and sweaty, my head's going to blow,
Everything around me is moving so slow.
I can't see or hear, please let it come back,
Enjoyment in life, is something I lack.

A loud thumping, I have a headache there,
All I can do is sit and stare.
Mouth feeling dry, I need something wet,
I find it hard to go and get.

Desperately need something cold to drink,
I'm too tired to even think.
Blood pressure is right down low,
It starts to rise when feelings go.

I am just glad when those feelings are gone,
I'm starting to think, what have I done wrong?
Hoping this fear will go away
Maybe happiness will soon come my way.

Beth Ralph

JUST AROUND THE CORNER

Just around the corner
A new day is due
How you enjoy it - is up to you

A lovely friend, a little treat
A cosy cafe, where loved ones meet

No-one knows what tomorrow will bring
But just around the corner
Suddenly - it's spring

Today is a memory
So short - but sweet
Tomorrow is another day
We have yet to meet.

Hazel Michell

THE EMPTY SWING

Sadly stands the empty swing
A lonely and neglected thing.
Where are the toys, there yesterday?
They now have all been put away.
The leaves are falling, crisp and brown
And dandelion clocks drift down.
Little feet are heard no more
On paths where they once trod before,
Little pegs on little line
No longer are put out with mine.
What happened to our happy hours?
Gone like summer's dying flowers.
Autumn's here and days grow cool,
My little one has started school.

Joyce Williams

RELATIVE DISTANCE

For eighteen months, the Sunday chats ensured
exchange of news, ills stoically endured,
the weather wanting. Yes, the kids are fine,
relatively speaking, up and down the line.

The journey done, acquaintance is renewed.
We sit, we talk, with strong tea freshly brewed.
The children, when enough is heard, are seen
and gently motioned towards the TV screen.

Talk tires soon with three more days to go
for catching up on all there is to know.
Now Countdown beckons on its daily run
Who can resist the final conundrum?

And later, brooding by the shingle shore
on age, and things that were and are no more;
cold flint compressed from countless marine lives
which man, in time, had fashioned into knives.

Our tools have given us the leading edge
Until we fall - or jump - from privilege.
What entities will view our flesh and bone
when we ourselves have settled into stone?

Alice Walsh

YOUR LITTLE PEOPLE

A child is something that is special,
Precious from the very start,
They are the special *little people*
That you love with all your heart.
When these little people get sick,
Sometimes, you stay up all night,
But that sweet little hug they give you,
Makes it worth it . . . right?
Of course little people become big people,
And ready to go on their way,
That's when you have to bite your tongue,
To keep from begging them to stay.
The only thing that makes it easier,
Is you know with them, they take your heart.
And until that special person returns,
The two of you will never really be apart.

Angela Winter

JOURNEY TO WORK

It started to rain,
Tee tee tee tum,
As I got on the train,
Tee tee tee tum.
Men in grey suits,
Tee tee tee tum,
Girls in high boots,
Tee tee tee tum,
Old ladies in hats,
Tee tee tee tum,
Boys in school caps,
Tee tee tee tum.
Soggy old coats,
Tee tee tee tum,
Good weather for boats,
Tee tee tee tum
No seats for us all
Tee tee tee tum,
See the rain fall,
Tee tee tee tum
The stench of damp cloth,
Tee tee tee tum
Can't wait 'til I'm off,
Tee tee tee tum.
But . . . when that magic time comes,
Tee tee tee tum,
Out comes the sun!
Tee tee tee tum.

Jasmine Roff

BEDTIME

When Mummy takes me up to bed,
And I have said my prayers,
She turns out the light, whispers goodnight
And slowly creeps downstairs.
I lie and look around the room
And try very hard to be brave,
But what is that shape up on my wall?
I'm sure it's a bear coming out of its cave.
And listen! What's that noise I hear?
It's like a lion's roar,
Maybe it's Daddy singing,
Or that ginger Tom next door.
I think I'll shout for Mummy,
She'll make them disappear,
But my eyes are getting heavy
And sleep is very near.
Then suddenly it's morning,
And the sun is everywhere.
I hear no lions roaring,
Or see no big black bear.
So I jump out of bed, feeling happy,
That everything's alright,
And I know I won't be scared,
When I climb in bed tonight.

Carol Bond

DREAMTIME ENCOUNTER

You didn't want me but you wanted my love
that I couldn't afford to give
or was it my insecurity and I couldn't get enough
to live and let live.
The sorrow collects in pools I wish you knew the depth
in my dream we bent the rules
our spirits met whilst I slept
I was naked and unashamed
running with no sense of direction
you were in the garden untamed on your own trajection.
We passed like old souls by the fountain
and went our separate ways
without regret or expectation,
in the rare realms of empty space
you came to me, then I saw your face,
our beings touched we needed no explanation.
Then we slipped back into our separate roles,
You were the inquisition, I was on the rack
You were burnt as a witch, I was heaping on the coals,
You were the hunter, I was the prey
You served me coffee in a roadside café,
You were the stranger, I was the priest
I was the guest at your wedding feast.

Paul Cobb

A Day In The Life

I listen to the wind as she blows
I listen to the rain as she pours
I see the sun as she rises
I see the moon at night
I see the stars shining bright
I see the snow fall in winter
I see it melt in the warmth of the sun
I have listened to the sound of the waves
I see boats floating by
I see seagulls flying high
I've seen the time on the clock go by
I hear people laughing
I see people who are sad
I've seen loved ones die
Old and young
I listen to Christmas carols being sung
I long to hear joyful people sing.

David O'Neill

BATTLE CRY

Upon this windswept hill I stand
With bloodied heart that stains my hand
As battle cries from distant hills
I stand and taste the bitter pills
Of hatred, love and honour.
We fight man to man, brother
against brother.
Why do we do it? When will it end?
Deep into battle, our menfolk we send.
Many years have now since passed
Has this battle been our last?
No more blood upon my hand
Upon this windswept hill, I stand.

J Rowley

SONG ON THE SAND

I met a man on local sand
He told stories and we sang all night
He played the banjo. The sea was his band
And I danced with the stars in delight
That night, now always further out of reach,
Comes to me in samples of memory song
But though the stranger's life still roams the beach,
Like the shards of broken jetsam, he has gone

I can't recall one word
Just an echo of placated sighs
It matters not what I heard
But what I caught of the night
And this is never out of reach
Like the samples of memory song.
And the stranger's life that roams the beach
Like the shards of broken jetsam, he has gone

My hand has risen alone in voice
Grains of chorus clutter through
Tired wind-trumpets of the past, rejoice
My lives are no longer two
Randomly, my soul creeps out to reach
Old samples of memory song
Again I touch the man who roams the beach
Though like shards of broken jetsam, he has gone

Carl Griffin

THE OLD MAN DOWN THE STREET

The summer's afternoon was hot and sticky.
The sun shone from a clear, blue sky.
Mary walked on without any hurry
Carrying three heavy carrier bags
Laden with groceries and presents too.
As she turned into the corner street,
A cheerful male voice said:
'Can I help you with a carrier bag?'
Mary stopped abruptly and looked to her right -
There stood an old man,
Smiling friendly from behind his gate.
She returned his friendly smile and said:
'Thank you, kind sir! But no, thank you!
However, I do appreciate your offer of assistance.'
'Oh please!' he begged, 'won't you let me help you?
I am feeble and old, that's very true,
But I am strong enough to help you through.'
Mary smiled friendly and began moving on,
Then stopped abruptly when he began to cry.
She slowly turned, gazing at him, quite puzzlingly.
'Please!' he began, his tone so tearful,
'I'll be ever so grateful if you'll only say yes!'
Smiling friendly, she nodded
Extending her hand with the carrier bag.
She stared with sheer amazement
At his sudden cheerful and pleasing smile.
'Thank you! Oh thank you!
For you've made my heart alight
Just letting me do a good turn
Me, this old man, down the street.'

Elsa Beggs

WHY?

So many questions within my mind,
So many emotions running inside.
So many feelings destroyed and yet
I wonder how everything changed, from first we met.

We met in the springtime, a number of years ago,
We loved each other truly and were so happy then, you know.
But, along the way, so many promises, hopes and dreams,
So many plans got destroyed to the extreme.

Many factors came into the equation,
Endless rows, differences and fears helped fuel the situation.
And then one day, you broke my heart,
It was then we knew we had to part.

Still, if I could wave a magic wand and travel back in time,
I'd have things as they were once, when they were 'yours and mine'.
Alas, time goes by - mistakes were made and things could
never be as before,
But the time we shared and the love we felt
will be there for evermore.

Carole-Anne Boorman

VENICE IN DISGUISE

Tied up, left deserted
they're lying side by side
like curvaceous bodies
which have ceased to glide
In this foggy gloom
the gondolas gently sway
obsolete, empty, dormant
silhouettes in grey
Quaint old bridges, abandoned, vacated
sweet arches dripping . . . isolated
An eerie sheen on cobblestones
a melancholic square
where pigeons are in hiding
atop the buildings fair
Someone passes fleetingly
has he an urgent task?
We shudder as we watch him
for the vision wears a mask
Would he be in 'disguise'
if the weather was clear
this jobless man, the punter
that hardy Gondolier
Where are you now Canal-man
are you back in your boat
and do you sing whilst you glide
now happily afloat?

Maria Johanna Gibbs

IMAGINE

Can you imagine a world that no longer has crime?
Where life is held precious, no one needlessly has to die.
For money, nor power - notoriety and fame,
Why is killing to some merely a sport or a game?

Imagine there is a world free of hatred and war,
No one has to die for an ill-gotten cause!
To those that sit on high - decide and break all our rules,
Instead of embracing peace, act like childish minded fools!

Imagine if you would, a world free from starvation and drought,
Where not one solitary soul has to go without.
Nor one single country, governs with power and greed,
They give to each subject; enough to drink and to feed.

Imagine in this world, love is what it should be,
The one and only true thing inside of you and of me.
An unconditional love, no one needn't pay for,
Neither to use, nor abuse: a love that forever is pure!

Imagine a world full of good, nil of evil and sin,
As it always should have been; our own Heaven on Earth.
Where no one need lose and for once you did win,
And no one ever was valued on material worth!

Why must one only imagine a world such as this?
Why cannot it be made real - that for so long has been missed.
The desire for a world where we truly belong,
Think me not as foolish - for how can it be wrong?
To wish to live in a world that already I'm sure,
Appears not to care for anyone any more!

Sean Michael Atherton

SOME FRIENDS

I thought we would forever be friends
but how wrong can one be?
I guess this is how it must be
no one seems to care, no one except me.
I thought if I tried hard enough
maybe they might see
But still nothing came, nor did anyone ring.
I waited day after day?
Each morning I would hope
but then as night drew near
My hope would turn to despair,
for they just do not seem to care.
All the things they said, the lies they told
what for, only they must know
For I still, three years on
have not given up hope.
I still sit in vain, hoping that my friends
of '97 will get in touch again.

Sarah Begum

FOREVER LOVE

You said it was for the best
that we went our separate ways,
So why do I have sleepless nights
and such painful days?
Your love to me was air
Which you would always give
but now that you've gone
I have no reason to live.
I've tried so hard
but you're still in my heart
Tormenting me with those memories
it feels as if we're not apart.
I remember those days
when we were always together.
Although your love for me is gone
I will still love you always and . . . forever.

Mohammed Asad

HURT

You've been patient, you've been kind,
trying to understand, and to help me.
Slowly going out of your mind,
. . . wondering how to make me see . . .
what is wrong with me?

Don't let me hurt you anymore,
I never meant for this to be.
Please let me go, but don't be sore,
It's for the best, don't you see . . .

Whatever you think, I've tried to be a good wife,
but that thing called love could not be found.
The only thing now is to get out of your life
Then once more, your friends can come around . . .

I thought I'd found this thing called love,
only to find it had tricked me again.
To me, you mean the world, but that is not love.
Sorry! I was wrong and caused you so much pain.

Don't let me stay here anymore
taking your life away . . .
Find a real love, it won't be hard,
For it's what should be, of that I am sure . . .

Roberta Pearson

THE VALUE OF LIFE

What are we at birth but the start of life itself
Of all the plans set out for health, happiness and wealth.

What are we in childhood but the demands our parents give
On how we act and how we think and how we are to live.

What are we in school years, but a child amongst the rest
Told to concentrate, absorb the knowledge, to always do our best.

What are we in adolescence, troubled, lost, confused,
Trying to find our path in life with all advice refused.

What are we in workforce, when our plans are put in place
When we take all life's to offer and it does become a race.

What are we when older as we settle for our lot
We look back at time passed by, are we pleased with what we've got?

What are we in death but a memory of our life
Of the times we've had both good and bad, of trouble stress and strife.

We are what we want to be, our life is in our hands
It's up to us to make it good and carry out our plans.

And when we've gone, if we've been good, honest, nice and kind
These will be the memories that we have left behind.

Susan Smith

FOR AMERICA

As the smoke and rubble settle
the reality becomes clear,
of those friends and relatives
that are no longer here.

A child's toy sits lonely
on a street where there's no sound,
then the rescue work begins
for those who are not yet found.

The enemy hides in shadows
the world unites as one,
the clean-up from this nightmare
has only just begun.

Let loved ones go towards the light
into arms of love,
and lay their heads upon the clouds
in the heavens above.

Anita Anthony

LEAVING

Starting 'big' school, I feel so grown up
Life is daunting and it's hard to cope
So many new faces, do I smile or not?
Will they respond, I'll give it a shot

Year 8 starts well, I know a bit more
Loads of great mates, good times in store
All the teachers are quite cool too
Oh, all except when the homework's due

Great news in Year 9, staying with Mrs B
She's more like a friend than a teacher, you see
More involved with the choir and I love to sing
Scully's my duet pal, we go with a zing

Year 10 gets serious, exams now hit
It's time to get down to the boring bit
Still having fun but working hard
With the boys in the band in the old school yard

That was quick, I can't believe it's passed
Year 11 has come round much too fast
One more year and no more school days
I seem to be walking round in a haze

It's here the day that just won't wait
The memories linger and the tears won't abate
I'll miss so many, faces dear
But there's no regrets, the future is here

Onto pastures completely new
I'll feel like a first-year, I won't have a clue
But with some familiar faces and old friends still there
I know I'll get by with new friends to share.

Shelagh Speakman

WORDS

Stories paint a vivid picture,
With written words so strong and pure,
Often though I sit and wonder,
How a sentence is formed at all.

By writers so silent, so deep in thought,
Their senses honed, yet words come forth,
How unfair that they are able,
To make a story or a fable.

Come to life so vividly,
And fill my mind with imagery,
Of dolphins gliding underwater,
And glades where glints of sunlight loiter.

Where twinkling raindrops shine and glisten,
And birds sing gaily if you listen,
Such magical letters linked together,
Is it trickery? No, writing is clever!

Am I worthy of such effort,
I ask as I read each sentence,
Yes, I truly believe I am meant to feel,
Each word as though it's actually real.

Page upon page of fascination,
Clips of a person's vivid imagination,
Sitting down, I soon move forward,
And sit in wonder of what lies ahead.

Will there be a trailing jungle,
Or a rhythmic elephant rumble?
Foreign lands or English shores,
What will the next page lead me towards?

Alas, the time for fun and adventure,
Has come to an end, but no matter,
It's time to create my own fantasies,
And dream the words for tomorrow's story.

L E Madgwick

HYPOCRITES

If there's a God, why do we cry?
Why would He separate the sea from the sky?
Fate throws misfortune, many must fight,
We'll ne'er be equal, 'cept under stars in the night.

For an ant underfoot, is guilt a pretence?
Why should we pray to omnipotence?
Society's morals were built on sufferance and pain,
You won't find a vegan on the African plain.

The savage reads nothing, won't have an eloquent grave,
But where would we be without 'savage slaves'?
While there were pyramids, Athens and Rome,
We picked at dirt in disease-ridden homes.

See the good people, front pews of the church,
All beautiful souls, but clouded by girth.
My life means decadence, comfort and mirth,
Two pounds a month? They'll inherit the Earth.

Pete Woods

PIPE DREAM

I feel there is a place for me
Along a road and down by the sea
It's a quaint little cottage, of that I'm sure
With a neatly thatched roof and roses round the door
The garden is full of sweet-smelling flowers
Where you can sit and relax for hours and hours.

I know that one day I'll find such a place
Then it won't take long to pack my case
I'll say goodbye to the city, the dirt and the fumes
And take a last look around my modern rooms
Leaving won't be a hardship for me
Cos I've always wanted a place by the sea.

Karen Dellow

PROGRESS

It's amazing the 'progress' that has been made over the last
sixty-odd years,
As for those of us born before 1940, I say to mankind a big 'Cheers.'
As we were born before television and videos, plastic, and
ballpoint pens,
Before North sea oil, Zerox, polio shots, artificial hearts and
contact lens . . .

There were no dishwashers, tumble-dryers, electric blankets or
group homes,
And no split atoms, laser beams, radar, satellites, or any
mobile phones,
We had no air conditioners, drip-dry clothing, disposable nappies,
or 'the pill',
And we existed before word processors, pagers, laptops, and house
husbands were nil . . .

In our day 'hardware' meant nuts and bolts and 'software' was not
even a word,
'Time sharing' meant togetherness, and pizzas and McDonald's were
names we never heard.
Most toilets were outside in the garden, and only the rich drove cars,
We were born before man walked on the moon, and soon it will
be Mars . . .

We got by without day centres, credit cards, yoghurt and lager -
what a shame,
And we thought 'sheltered accommodation' was where we waited
for a bus in the rain,
And 'going all the way' was staying on the train till the end of the line,
And a 'garden centre' was the middle of the garden, and 'the net' was
for fishing - that's fine . . .

We did not have supermarkets, motorways, holidays abroad, and a lot, lot more,
And counselling for stress . .. 'tea and a Woodbine' . . . was all we got in the war,
But a lot of us survived without all these things, as a hardy bunch were we,
So what will it be like in sixty years time? I'm afraid we won't be here to see . . .

Bryan J Anthony

THANK GOD FOR MAKE-UP

'Thank God for make-up' she thought to herself
As she gazed at the bottles
Lined up on the shelf

Creams to hide blemishes
Creams to fill cracks
Creams to replace what the body now lacks

Lotions and potions
Face packs and then
A remedy to make us look young again

Lipstick, mascara, eye shadow too
Blushers, foundation
To name but a few

Eyeliner, lip gloss, a big powder puff
Brushes and pencils
You can't have enough

Smoothing the crow's feet
Disguising the bags
She had no intention of being a hag

A little assistance to help keep her youthful
(More than a little
If she were truthful)

An hour-long ritual but hey, what the heck
She had to smooth out
That turkey-like neck

Blow being natural, she wasn't a saint
And no one would know her
Without her war paint

All these solutions lined up on the shelf
Thank God for make-up
She thought to herself.

Jane Lynch

THE STRANGER

She doesn't know this woman
She has suddenly become,
Who blooms like a flower opening
To the warmth of the summer sun.

She doesn't know this woman
Whose heart is filled with song.
Who smiles at a secret happiness
And dreams the whole day long.

She doesn't know a meeting
Of kindred souls can be,
A melting of minds and bodies
In an exquisite harmony.

She doesn't know the touch of lips
Can turn the blood to fire,
And soft caressing fingers
Arouse such hot desire.

She doesn't know someone will come
And call her to awake;
To offer her the cup of love
From which her lips will take.

She doesn't know of the magic spell
One sip from the cup will cast,
But unsought comes the certainty
Of its power to hold and last.

She doesn't know; she doesn't know
How fair this Earth will be,
When life unfolds once more to her
Its wondrous mystery.

She cannot see the future years
Which only time can show,
When she'll rejoice in learning all
The things she doesn't know.

Ann Jarvis

STATE OF MIND

The air was clean
And the grass was green
As I walked along the road
All I could say was -
'I'm happy today'
And in my face it showed.

Many people would agree
You only see what you want to see
And that day
There was no grey
The sun was shining in the sky
And a cloud looked lonely as it floated by.

Spring flowers peeped out from the ground
So I tried not to make a sound
But the birds didn't feel as I
The songs they sang were shrill and high
I love the spring, life starts anew
This is no time to feel down and blue.

Kaye Coomber

UNTITLED

Little children all around
Lying like rags upon the ground
Bellies, swollen eyes, are sore
What's God doing this for?
Or is it man with his greed
Who'd rather have gold than the seed?
Bellies swollen with food and wine
Always going out to dine
These men will live their wondrous lives
Till their bodies rot and die
Then they'll suffer more than these
That were tortured for their needs.

Donna Easter

LADDERS

The crack in the curtains lets in the sun, invading the darkness
                                                    surrounding me.
An unwelcome reminder that there is a world outside this room.
Everyone is climbing a ladder, it's as simple as a cat climbing a tree,
but everyone has a ladder, everyone except for me.
The people outside have their worries, their own crosses they
have to bear,
but they live safe in the knowledge that their ladders are always there.

Some quickly reach the top, their achievements clearly show,
others at the bottom know their progress will be slow,
those in the middle are caught between the two,
knowing if they miss a rung they may not see it through,
but if they believe and gradually take their time,
they will succeed and reach the top, they have a chance, where is mine?

How did they get their ladders that help them deal with life?
The rungs to see them through heartbreak, depression and daily strife?
Where do they find the courage after a severe blow,
to start climbing those rungs once more, to have another go?

The accident that took him from me left no scars that show,
but guilt, grief and constant pain refuses to let me go.
The vision of seeing him suffering, in such obvious distress,
and slowly losing his life, why is anyone's guess.

I hope there is a ladder somewhere inside of me,
the hard part is finding it and then setting it free.
I must accept that I will fall but pick myself up,
allow others to help and know when to rest or stop.

I will begin to search for my ladder,
and a future that is not bleak but bright,
and I will start today by drawing back the curtains, letting in the light.

Melanie E Carty

MY BIRDS

I watch wild birds from my window
Five starlings, two sparrows and a crow
They come every day without fail
Three blue tits and the odd wagtail

It is nice to hear their early morning call
All trying to get one large seed ball
It makes me smile on a cold, rainy day
To watch all of them fight and play

Their table manners are not great
But for their meals they are not late
They all line up upon a great big tree
And they never seem to be afraid of me.

P Shallcross

TOBY

You came into our lives
When you were just a pup
You took over the house
And mucked everything up

Now you're an adult
You're just the same
You rule the roost
And put everyone to shame

He's kind and he's gentle
And he wouldn't hurt a fly
Well, maybe that part
Is a bit of a lie

He chases away cats
And teases other dogs
He also runs away
With everyone's socks

His name is Toby
And he's a bundle of fun
He's a Staffordshire cross
And he weighs a ton.

Rose Farman

THE BEAUTIFUL SNOW

The crisp snow floated steadily down
hitting and sticking to holy prepared ground
it is the Lord's will
for us to see His wonders still

When all is laid, it carpets the earth
snow-covered streets lined the town with value and worth
the crystals looked like jewels glistening
but to God's voice not many listening

Some see it as a time to play
let's make a snowman before it goes away
others saw God's handiwork and praised
look what He has done, at His creation we are amazed

Then came the thaw at His hands too
some moan and are angry and blue
oh the inconvenience of it all
it may even cause some to fall

Now that the crystal jewels have gone
each one unique in its own beauty shone
all that is left is the black ice and slush
thanks for the experience, thank you very, very much.

Jean M Grant

LOVE'S PHILOSOPHY

The fountains mingle with the river and the rivers with the ocean
The winds of Heaven mix for ever and ever with sweet emotions
The heavenly commotion, a Godly potion of love embracing with
                                            the sea and the ocean.

Johanna Isobella Brooks

POST PERSON'S LAMENT

I am but a postman delivering the mail to you,
through all kinds of weather, this is true.
I have met some great people as I do my rounds,
what a great job this would be if it wasn't for the hounds,
they sit behind the letter box, just waiting for me,
then try to bite my fingers off or have a dammed good chew.

As I walk around the streets another hound I am sure to meet,
when he runs at me at thirty miles an hour, jumping, barking
and growling, makes me feel very sour.
If I try to defend myself the hound will go berserk,
then the owner will come out and say, 'Leave my dog alone, you jerk!'

If dog owners only realised I am only trying to do my job,
it is their responsibility to keep control of their dog.
So please my dear friends, remember it is up to you,
if you keep your dog under control, I will deliver your mail safely
to you.

Kenneth Foster

LOVE CONQUERS ALL

Love is good, love is pure, love is all around
But for some I fear the worst for love cannot be found
These loveless souls can do no right
For all they do is argue and fight.
Surely nature cannot be to blame?
It's only people that can fan this evil flame.
What is to be done about this disgrace
That's thrust upon our human race?
To find a cure that is a 'must'
Before we turn our world to dust.
It's not too late I hope and pray
Someone is born again to show us the way.
So let's stop banging our head against the wall
And show that love can conquer all.

A Wilcox

THE BOX OF MEMORIES

Open the box and look inside
Lo and behold what can you see?
I see summer days and blue skies above
Children's voices laughing as they run to the cool blue sea

Look again and what do you see?
My lovely mum before she was ill
With love in her eyes just for me

I grasp her hand but she's not there
Quick shut the box, the pain's too much to bear

Think of the future to grandchildren in store
Laughing and playing in the cool blue sea
Turn the key to the box
Maybe the pain will ease.

L Whitehouse

SPRING

The land is changing its wintry face.
A new season upon us, spring is taking its place.
The birds are singing, there are lambs in the field.
The weather is warming, green are the hills.
Crocuses, tulips, blossom on the trees.
Daffodils blooming for us to see.
The earth is awakening, the birds, how they sing
They all want to tell us, 'Here is the spring.'

The creatures are stirring from their long winter's sleep
Rubbing their eyes, just taking a peep.
To look around them, all bathed in sunlight.
To them it's such a glorious sight
The birds are gathering twigs for their nests.
Twittering, chirping, the time they like best.
This is the season that makes my heart sing.
For gone is the winter and here is the spring.

Lynne Clements

THE STORM

The storm it rages, the thunder roars,
The waves are lashing on the shores.
The wind is howling round the mast,
How much longer can our little ship last?
She's taken a battering from the hail,
Will she make port or ride the gale?

She's been a good ship but she's getting old,
Now she's being tossed and rolled.
The crew's not rested now for days.
Her master on the bridge he stays,
Trying to keep her straight and true
Hoping to save his ship and crew.

The waves, they smash upon the deck,
The wheel house now has become a wreck.
Our ship, it battles in the foam
Heading for our port and home.
It's still a way to safety yet,
But we will make it, our mind is set.

The dawn, it breaks, the sky is clear,
We're nearly home, we've nothing to fear.
Our engine is damaged, we're struggling on,
We've fought a battle and we've won.
The lights of the harbour can now be seen
Not far away upon our beam.

Now we're in the harbour and we've made fast,
Our master has brought us to safety at last.
His devotion to duty, he saved his men,
When his ship is repaired, he'll do it again.
To all of our seamen, wherever they be
Good luck, go with you, sail on a calm sea.

C W Gosling

SLEEP

Sleep is life
Sleep is death
Sleep is like a single breath
Falling through that deep black hole
To the place that soothes your soul

Drawn up to the nether plane
With dark blue clouds
And yellow rain
The ageless child
The huge green fly
Jumping up to swim the sky

Try to touch
Try to feel
Knowing that it's all so real
Floating free up to the sun
Dropping down until we run

We laugh, we cry
In dreams we keep
We float in life
We float in sleep.

J Doolan

INNOCENCE WILL BE REBORN

Forget the adults' politics,
Fight for the children's innocence

So that as they grow and learn,
They will pass it on in turn

Innocence, a gold braid thread,
Like ancient wisdom words still said

Forget some adults' twisted lies,
Petty fights, insane crimes.

Fight? Yes, fight my friend!
For innocence you may not see again

Many children have it stolen away,
Beaten, hurt, tears wrenched all day -
Some kids' lives are painted grey

Friendly flowers, a hand in the snow,
It's only love that makes children grow

So grow sweet child, grow so tall!
You have mountains to move as evil empires fall

They'll fall!

Down to dust,
Of electrical TV programmed rust

And love will rekindle innocence lost
As every spark of love means it surely must.

David M Jesse

A Special Friend

Years of friendship we shared together,
Stay in my thoughts and heart forever,
Used to talk and laugh for hours
I send you my love with these flowers.
Take good care of her God above
And shower her with kindness, tenderness and love.

Gillian Guard

THE TUDORS

The Tudors were a likely bunch
With their tales of sadness and woe,
But when it comes down to the crunch
Of them what is really known?

For all that was written in the books
By ancient authors of Britain,
One man's myth or lie was mistook
And the truth, very rarely, thus written.

The bygone age was of strange indifference
During those days so long ago,
Communications of no existence
Or they took many moons to show.

Death was a daily fact of life
Around which many a book was set,
For to use the wrong words and deprive,
The final sentence the author would get.

So many a story has been distorted
To suit the king at the top,
Take lightly all which has been reported,
Produced so the tongues would stop.

Historians all do not believe
The tales which have been portrayed,
The Crown of Roses was perceived,
But the true faith was not slayed,

And one day hence if he should decide
To bring them back into this life,
The Tudors will look to God to guide
Their continuance free of strife.

Julia Kelly

A Witchy Tale

I hear the wolves among the trees, a chill runs down my spine
I'm off to see the wise old witch whose wisdom will be mine
Darkness falls, the silence grows, I must be moving on
The moon above lights up the sky, dark clouds have scurried on
The witch I see within her cave with lanterns all aglow
Black bats abound, hang upside down with wings that seem to grow
She looks my way, I start to stare
Her eyes are green, she has black hair
Her books of spells lie on the ground
Her old black cat makes purring sounds
Her voice is soft, 'Come, sit with me,
I'll teach you well, just wait and see.'
We cast our spells until the dawn
I'm now a witch, I've been reborn.

Cynthia Davis

PLEASE DON'T ASK

Please don't ask me to say 'Sorry,'
You know I find this tough,
I'd sooner let dust settle, though to you this may seem rough.

Please don't ask me to say 'Thank you,'
You know I find this hard,
I'd sooner seem ungrateful (so don't expect a card).

Please don't ask me if I love you,
You know I'm rather shy,
I'd sooner be a fortress watching missed loves pass me by.

Please don't ask me how my life is,
You know I'd only lie,
I'd sooner tell you 'Things are great,' then whilst alone I'd cry.

Please don't ask me how I'll end this,
You know I've not a clue,
But I'll leave you with the thought that every word I've said is true!

Jonathan M Everingham

SOMETHING MY DAUGHTER SAID

I don't want to work at Sainsbury's
wearing that 'orrible blue dress
sorting out the cabbages
the carrots and the cress

I don't want to be an air hostess
wiv me feet hardly touching the ground
or serve customers at Milletts
to clothe the outward bound

I don't want to sweep up hair
that people do not want
or model clothes
in the style of Mary Quant

I don't want to be a happy smiley nurse
dispensing to all that are not well
or be a lady poet
if the words they do not gel

I'd rather sit at home
watching soaps upon me telly
than go out to work
to pay for food that's in me belly.

Vernon Ballisat

WAS IT ALL A LIE?

Everything I ever believed in
Has come crashing around my head
Moments I thought were monumental
Turn out to be nothing more than lies instead

I was an everyday man
A teacher earning his pay
Now I am on this soldier's playground
Trying just to live one more day

Was I here to defend my country?
To lay down my life if need be?
No, I am never going to kill anyone
I just try to stop them killing me

I sit on my knees in the water
Blurred figures to my left and right
I wash my helmet of its bloodied content
While a limbless soldier still tries to fight

Around me they fall and keep falling
A swarm of bodies known only by a chain
We step on the foothpath of possible death
Are we heroes or simply insane?

Jo Hayton

I'm Breathing Again

I'm living, I'm breathing,
I'm happy again.
I look in the mirror
And I see me again.
There's a real person inside of me
Can you see it, the real me?
I've been dead inside for much too long
But now I know I can sing my song
You can hear my voice
You can catch my eye
I'm living now, it is my chance
And you're right, yes, I'm going to dance!

Jane Wilkinson

RETURN TO ME

Return to me, though long has been the time
Since hearts and minds were touched with signs of spring
Now in the fiery glow of autumn leaf
Return to me, for you are mine

Through the long avenues of time
O'er many a tumbling, rushing stream
My voice will ever call the wanderer home
Return to me for you are mine

Return to memories of past times
To dreams and scenes of long ago
Return to feel and love, and live again
Come back to me, for you are mine.

Wesley Stephens

LONELY

Here again I lie in my empty bed. Secluded from the outside.
Only thoughts of love I never had, keep me from falling into an
everlasting sleep.

Here I lay with thoughts abound
Heart pounding with passion, for
The love I've never found

So much to give
So much to share
Yet there's no one ever there.

In my nakedness I lay
The thoughts of perfection
My mind surveys

If I should die
While I'm asleep
I'm sure my life
Would be complete

But in the morning
When I wake
My life again
Will take this fate

No one here to hold me tight
No one to love or kiss goodnight
Oh when, oh when, can I share my love
With that special someone I'm dreaming of?

Not today I'll have to wait, but some day soon I'll meet my mate.

Sherland Boyce

WHAT IS LOVE?

Love is wonderful, it brings laughter and joy,
Love can be hurtful, can bring pain and sorrow,
How can something so wonderful be so bad
How can love make you so happy but also so sad.

What is love? Is it good?
How can such a wonderful thing hurt so much?
It makes you laugh, then you feel sad,
The love which felt so good, suddenly makes you feel bad,
Love puts you on a high, then makes you sit back and sigh,
Love at times will make you curl up and want to cry.

Love is so strong, it is a powerful source
When it happens
You lose all control
Happy one minute,
Next so sad
Love, what is it?
If you have found it,
You should be glad.

What is love? Is it good?
How can such a wonderful thing hurt so much?
It makes you laugh, then you feel sad,
The love which felt so good, suddenly makes you feel bad,
Love puts you on a high, then makes you sit back and sigh,
Love at times will make you curl up and want to cry.

Some people never find this thing called love,
If you have, give thanks to above,
As you are lucky to experience it,
Good or bad, it is worth it.

Jennifer Park

SEASONS OF CHILDHOOD

Spring was full of April showers
And birds made a wonderful sound
Bluebells, daisies and buttercups
Grew in abundance all around

Summer and the sun was hot
It made bubbles in the tar
We walked in the road to pop them
With no fear of any car

Autumn, when the leaves fell
They made a rustling sound
And settled on the ground below
Like a carpet on the ground

Winter and the snow was deep
Or so to me it seems
Are these seasons of my childhood
Or is it only in my dreams?

It doesn't really matter
If they were bad or good
We all know that we really loved
The seasons of our childhood.

Maureen Millar

DISASTER

Standing at the pit-head
In the quiet, quiet dawn,
Wives and sweethearts silent
On this bitter, senseless morn.
Mothers, fathers, cousins
Searching for their own,
Peering at each stretcher
With a soulful, silent moan.
Rescue teams reluctant
Feared of what they'll see,
Blackened, grimy faces
Bring up a young trainee.
Frantic prayers go soaring
'Please let my son survive,'
And there he goes by limping
Battered, but alive.
But soon relief becomes dismay
And tears begin to run,
Shed for the lifeless body
Of some other mother's son.

Marie Gray

GREEN EYES

Your eyes are indescribable,
They're as beautiful as can be,
With every look,
I see a different depth in you,
As you slowly take over me.

Your lips are irresistible,
If I should get just one taste,
I'd savour every moment of . . .
Our passionate and warm embrace,
There's not a single second,
I would want to waste.

Your mind is so desirable,
I cherish every thought you share,
How have I not known you for so long?
To me that's just unfair.

Basically, you are indescribable, so desirable
and irrestisible to me,
I hope one day I know,
What it is I can do,
So that a guy like me,
Can be with a girl like you!

Matthew Tushingham

LIFE'S OPPOSITES

Our memories were happy,
Our memories were sad,
Some of the times were good,
Some of the times were bad,
We could feel things were so wrong,
We could feel things were so right,
Many times from darkness
Would often come the light,
Ours was the right to say yes,
Ours was the right to say no,
We found our days would come,
We found our nights would go,
To win, to lose, we couldn't always choose,
Human life begins,
Then human life must end,
The things I write about,
Are what's in-between my friend.

Fiona Bhatia

MUM

What is your birthday in Heaven really like?
Do you have presents, candles and cake?
And is God sitting by your side
Granting every wish you make

'Cause you know if that's true
What my wish would be
If anything could be mine
And that wish would be
To spend your birthday with you
And help you blow your candles out
Just one more time

I hope your day is as special as can be
Because God took you for His angel
When you should have been with me

You're in my thoughts
Night and day
And I miss you so much
The pain never goes away
I'm asking myself why life is so unfair
A child needs a mother that will always be there

Happy birthday, Mum
I know you're watching from above
And every time I think of you
My heart is filled with love.

Simone Fontana

IMAGINE IF OUR MEN

Imagine if babies were bore by our men,
Oh what a panic we would 'ave then,
Imagine if labour came on Saturday afternoon,
Imagine his face, 'The match kicks off soon.'

Imagine if it came Sunday night
As he stands at the bar sippin' his pint
Imagine his face if his waters did break
'What happens now, for Heaven's sake?'
'Oh come on now love, one mighty push
Get a move on, babe, before last orders' rush.'
Imagine, imagine, is all we can say,
Our men having babies? Don't think so, no way!

Donna Brade

ODE TO A MOTHER

I guess you never thought
That you would hear from me
You thought that all those years ago
What would be would be -
I dreamt of what you looked like
Were you beautiful and kind?
Or did I really matter
Did you cast me from your mind?
Did you think of me as I grew up?
Did you think how it felt for me
Not knowing where I belonged
Not knowing the real me?
Did you wonder if I'd married?
Did you think if I had a career?
Did you ever stop to think of me
Feel guilty, shed a tear?
So I'm asking you the question
Am I everything you thought I would be?
Do you wish you'd been there all my life
Spent time with the real me?
Can you ever make up for the time gone by?
Could you be a real mother to me?
I think it's a case of too little too late
Cause I've managed so far you see
But I'll always be grateful you gave me a life
I've achieved and made my dreams come true
Now I'm married with children and a beautiful wife
I could never have done this without you.

Michael McLaughlin

CHILDREN OF A LESSER GOD
(For the children of Africa)

Images keep taxing my mind
Is this the face of mankind?
Tears frozen amidst the blazing sun
Miles of path, nowhere to run
Dust quietens unheard sighs
Dare I glimpse in their eyes?
Pain puts a barrier clouding their emotion
Happiness . . . a far-fetched notion
Hope shrouded by painful moans
No energy to echo any groans
A generation has passed
A generation will pass
Feeling the pain of a lost childhood
Drifting into an old age without an adult stage
We have everything
They have nothing
My cup overflows
Their cup is non-existent
My heart is aching
Who do I blame in this making?
Why dear God
But why this mode?
Or are they the children of a lesser God
Forgotten in strife
Abandoned in life?

Naina Mehta

A Letter To My Instincts

Please be my breast-plate, my guard for the fight.
Be my inner strength and be my true might.
Please be there for me and be my strong tower.
Please give me hope and everlasting power.

Please be my vision and be my true word.
Make me have the freedom and fly high as a bird.
Please give me courage when I need it the most.
Help to believe I believe in us both.

When I am feeling restless, please calm me down.
Give me a life buoy for my guilt, so in my
Conscience I will never drown.

I owe a lot to you in my life and things I thought I couldn't achieve.
You gave me self-respect, reason to believe.
You are the voice that goes on inside my head.
The one that doesn't keep quiet and wishes I was dead.

You are the feeling that lies deep inside my heart.
That gives the ray of light that lights up my dart.
Sometimes I feel I don't want you in my life.
When I want to forget the repercussions of the
Things I do, that always give me strife.

You were with me in the beginning and with me in the end too.
No one understands how I feel or what I see except you.
For you are my impulses and instincts, my uncertainty.
I will forgive you for all you have done,
Because hey, you are just me.

B M Wheaton

THE SUNSET

The beach is almost empty at the fading of the sun.
The gushing Scottish surf the only sound.
The golden sands of Ayre are pure and fine as dust
With darker patches where the night gains ground.

Across the glistening silver sea the Isle of Arran looms.
And at this time when day is nearly done
The brilliance of the sky is quite breathtaking
And the island bathes in the glow of the setting sun.

And as the sun sinks lower, a blazing ball of fire
With red and orange tendrils stretching wide.
It slips slowly behind Arran's sheltering mountains
With only the hand of nature as its guide.

W A Ronayne

UNTITLED

The sun's gone in, the lights are dim,
the kids are now asleep.
Why does the woman in the chair
whisper as she weeps?

Her love has gone, he passed away,
no time to say goodbye.
Her whispers turn to screams and shouts
of why? Why? Why?

She drifts to sleep and dreams of him,
their love is strong and free.
But when she wakes the nightmare's back,
she's lonely, sad and weak.

The children hear their mother's cries,
and no longer can they rest.
They huddle round her with their love,
and snuggle to her breast.

She strokes their hair and sings to them,
a soothing lullaby.
The night has passed, the sun is up,
another day to cry.

Days and months have passed her by,
days and months that she has cried.
A year has passed and she still asks,
Why? Why? Why?

Kim Mardell

MUM

Our perfect mum is small and sweet
She always looks pretty and neat
She has fluffy white hair and soft, soft skin
These are the things that make our hearts sing

Our perfect mum

Warm and gentle, soft and mild, gentle to
the touch as you brush her cheek

Our perfect mum

She loved her girls and her grandchildren too
But most of all Dad she loved you

Our perfect mum

Rest in peace Mum, on your final journey
From each of us, you take a piece of our hearts
Keep them safe with you, for surely one day
We will meet again
And you will make us whole again

Our perfect mum

Marion Morgan

SETTING OUT

The wind blows so cold
As we set out so bold
We snuggle up close
Wiggle our toes.
Soon will be spring
And no need for these things
Look forward to summer
To cast off our throws.
We'll still snuggle up close
And wiggle our toes
As we set out so bold.

P Wilde

FIERCE

A fierce temper rises then ebbs away.
There's no telling when it will appear or what it will make me say.
Some desperate pain hidden deep inside, not knowing the cause,
No excuse to provide.
I scream, I shout, hurt, only finding peace when I become so
                                            quiet and introvert.
At first a naughty child, then teenage moods, now a young adult
Trying to contain this fierceness, this attitude.
An angry temper rises then ebbs away.
My sharp tongue lashes out cutting anyone that would stay.
This time I'm forgiven as ever before, but one day they'll stop
The forgiving and close all the doors.

Mariama Abenaa Amoah

FAIRYLAND

It was an enchanted secret, special in a way
They all came out at once, for lots of fun and play
How beautiful they looked, upon this summer night
Sparkling pretty colours, shining oh so bright
The fairies as they came, tiptoeing on the ground
Out of trees and hollows, magic can be found
The tingling in the air, the thought that they are free
Streaming through the valley, where no one else could see
Leaping, hopping, skipping, dancing as they go
Starting to get faster now, flying high and low
Ducking, diving, weaving, their wings are very grand
Whatever is this place? This could be fairyland
Fairy houses and toadstools, is this really true?
Do you believe in fairies? I know that I do
Step in a fairy ring, you'll see what it's about
But just remember if you do, you never can climb out

Z J Thomas

IN MEMORY OF ROVER

We walk no more with Man-dog
Through the meadows and the park
No more we see his waving tail
Or hear his joyous bark
He sniffs no more the thistles
Or frolics in the hay
He waits no more to greet us
As we homeward wend our way.

For many long and happy years
He worked around the farm
Every inch of land he knew
Every rat hole round the barn
He sniffed each rabbit warren
As he slowly wandered by
Often he would chase them with
His happy yelping cry.

His later years he spent in quiet rest
With those he loved and those who loved him best
He went for walks, he sat and watched
Quite often he just dozed
Until the day those big brown eyes were gently closed.

Sleep here in peace within this quiet spot
Where roses grow and blue forget-me-not
You served us well through all the years
'Twas very sad your life should have to end
Old Rover dog, you were our faithful friend.

Eric Humphries

JUST NEEDED TO SAY

I know that all this mushy stuff
Just isn't quite your scene
But there's something I need to say
About how wonderful you've been.

This time of year five years ago
All my dreams were shattered
But you were there to help me see
Just what really mattered.

You helped me to be positive
About the years ahead
And kept what was really worrying you
Left unsaid.

I know you find it painful
And sometimes you get scared
But I'm really doing fine now
And all because you cared.

There's not a lot that I can say
To make up for what you've done
But we have the rest of our lives to enjoy
Now that the battle's been won.

This poem's full of meaning
With a loving message to say
You really mean the world to me
And I'll always feel this way.

So to put an end to what I've said
The words are very few
All I want to say right now
Is, 'Darling I love you . . .'

Diane Burgess

THE SPACE BESIDE ME VAN!

There's a piece of ground that I 'ave found
that's oh so full of weeds
with lots of grass and strips of soil but 'ardly any trees.
I took it in hand, sat and planned
the course I'd have to take.
First I'll need a fork, a spade, then a rake.

The day arrives, I give a sigh at the task that lies ahead.
No more daisies or dandelions,
and no more lying in bed.
Early mornings came and went,
with heaps of money that I have spent.

The sun has come along with gales,
followed by the rain.
I've been burnt, wet and blown,
it's driven me insane.
My back has ached, my bones have cracked,
but it's worth it to hear people say,
'Look at that!'

Now winter's on its way,
the winds have come in force.
They've battered the trees, upset the leaves,
and blown down my fence, of course.

Amongst the mess the storms have left,
are many broken hearts.
But not long now 'til spring comes round,
and once again I'll start.

Sofi

A PIT LAD'S LOT

A rat's small eye is passing by
glued to the bag wherein there lies
my bait of bread and cheese
for in a tunnel I do creep on water covered knees
on and on I ply my way
- there is no turning back
for far beneath the North Sea's bed
this pit lad's working to be fed;
on and on he drills his day
for a wagon full of coal and a packet of pay

I dream of my sweetheart - I think of her hair
as its gold lights her pillow - as she lays lying there
her sweet face smiling she is waiting for me
six miles under a seabed - six miles under the sea
just a lad in a coal mine, who will work out this day
for a wagon full of coal - and a packet of pay

Far below beneath hillside - beneath Earth's molten rock
beneath valley - and sea - this poor pit lad will knock
knocking ten times his dozen - knocking ten times his score
beneath waves that are crashing he will hew even more
and I'll come home so weary will this pit miner's son
I won't finish this shift - till this bargain's been done
just a lad in a coal mine who works out his day
for a wagon full of coal and a packet of pay

Diana Mullin

LIFE IN THE FORTIES

Life in the forties was hard for us all.
Cold in the winter, grey paint on the walls.
Candles flickering in tin candlesticks.
Tilly lamps burning with thin tapered wicks.

Washing hanging from ceiling to floor.
Dark brown paint that's chipped on the door.
Blankets at windows to block out the light.
Coats on the bed to warm you at night.

The wireless crackling with news of war.
Doodlebugs sounding, all down on the floor.
Ration books needed for all that we bought.
Nothing was purchased without careful thought.

Fingers were tingling without any gloves.
Cuddling up closely like young turtledoves.
The summers were hot, over fields we did go
Down to the stream to dip in your toe.

Fishing for tiddlers in jam jars with string.
If you had a catch you felt like a king.
Home up the hill who would be first?
Stopping at times tar bubbles to burst.

Hunks of hot bread all smothered in jam.
Later for tea, mashed potato and Spam.
Tucked up in bed real tight to the wall.
Maybe life wasn't so bad after all.

C Rains

QUESTIONS

At sweet sixteen, not yet a lady
but pretty as a snow-white dove,
you looked at me and asked, so sweetly,
'Will I ever fall in love?'

I dropped the book that I was reading
and looked for guidance from above.
Yet, you persisted with another,
'Have you ever been in love?'

And, then, I went away to college.
The parting brought us such sweet pain.
It's my turn, now, to ask the question,
'Will we love this way again?'

Crystal Gene Nicholas

CHILDISH

The decision is to leave, the compulsion is to stay.
We should take a chance on life, we should throw caution away.
I see an old age pension.
I see a married life.
I fear the boredom of becoming some dull and kind man's wife.
I see his sweet young children, a mother's role I cannot play.
The time I have upon this Earth is getting shorter by the day.
I wish my views were more unselfish, I wish my soul was more
Enlightened, but like a lost young child I'm so fearful and
                                                    so frightened.

Abby Feast

THAT FIRST LOOK

I stand transfixed and look into those eyes
Who see all truth, reflect my very soul
And I see there a world so fresh and wise.
Before the mire of *life* can take its toll.

I must reach out my hand . . . a soft caress
Wanting so much to comfort and to care,
Lost in the wonder of that steady gaze,
The faith and trust, the family ties we share.

No artifice, no trick of lens or light
Can match this pure perfection . . . I am sure,
Here is the essence, here is the meaning of my life,
And after all these years, I love once more.

What price our transient wealth, possessions, land?
Nothing could be for me so great a prize,
As the sweet promise of our hope and joy,
When first we look into our grandchild's eyes.

E W Mills

TWILIGHT YEARS

They say age is only a number but I disagree,
I know cos it's inevitable and it's happened to me.

No more late nights or you pay the next day,
No more late meals or digestions affray.

Stairs are now taken just one at a time
Not two and a run, as in your prime.

Eyesight is monitored on much regular base,
Lines appear daily changing contours of face.

Bending's an effort and housework's a chore,
Chewing's a problem - and there's much more.

But there are concessions - travel, theatre and all
And so these should be, with income so small.

But age brings us wisdom, patience and grace,
A slowing enjoyment, life's no longer a race.

Memories give pleasure as never before
And time is more precious with those you adore.

So, life's what you make it and I'm making mine
And praying to God that I'll have lots more time.

S Daykin

GONE BUT NOT FORGOTTEN

When God took you to Heaven,
You were only fifty-seven.
Why did you have to die?
Did he want another angel in the sky?

The blow was hard, the shock severe,
To part with one, we loved so dear.
No words can be spoken,
Our hearts are broken.

Whenever you were asked for advice,
You would give it without thinking twice.
You leave behind 2 daughters and a wife,
Who, with our help can carry on with life.

You were my brother-in-law,
To me you were much more.
You were like a brother to me,
I am so sorry this parting had to be.

Those who you loved and met,
Are the ones who cannot forget.
Our loss is great, we cannot explain,
Goodbye, until we meet again.

When God took you home to rest,
He took away the very best.
Good night and God bless.

Margaret Griffiths

UNTITLED

Distant faces, forgotten faces,
Folk that I once knew,
Come to life, awaken me,
As the morning light breaks through.
Could it be so long ago,
The fun and frolics in the snow,
Our summer nights spent on the sand,
As you danced away to your favourite band,
For friends have forgotten, the way they'd sworn,
To be there always, request on demand,
If you ever needed that helping hand.
As one by one the numbers dwindled,
Faded memories remain, fewer thoughts rekindled.
They'd promise to write. To visit, to phone,
But you end up sitting all alone.
The passage of time,
Will rob you of some,
Others will fade,
The cowards just run.
Solidarity reigns, in this solitary brain,
My best friend am I,
Who's never the twain.

Syd Saeed

SPRING

The gloomy days of winter are fading fast,
And the glowing light of spring is in sight,
Sap is rising and trees burst their buds at last,
Dawn is breaking and the sun begins to shine,
What joy to be alive this wonderful day,
To arise and start the day feeling fine,
The wonders of nature what more can one say.
The soft warm breeze blowing through the trees,
Like sweet music on the early morning air,
The sound of the busy working bees
Flitting from flower to flower with great care,
Blossom on the trees a sight to behold,
Filling the air with a perfume so sweet,
Daffodils blooming in a blaze of gold,
The lawns freshly mown and looking neat.
When shadows fall and their day is ending,
Flowers close their petals and start to rest,
Night covers all and the moon is shining
On trees reaching to the sky, looking their best.

To stroll in Richmond Park
Among bracken standing high,
Fine oak trees with gnarled bark,
Branches reaching to the sky.
Deer grazing peacefully
On grass with the glistening dew.
Birds singing merrily,
Singing a song sweet and true.
Ducks on the pond so proud,
The sound of rippling water.
Blue skies without a cloud,
Come spring, summer and winter.

L R Jennings

WITH YOU

First experiences I got,
when we met each other.
Do you remember? My God!
I don't want to find another.

Pictures I have, memories too,
What about you?
I miss you, I hope; you too,
I'd like to stay with you.

I felt so happy beside you,
still I feel emotion,
pampering, passion and devotion,
of course, with whom?
                    With you!

Roberto León-Miranda

WHEN THEY'RE GONE

When they finally lay to rest
Was their life really just a test?
Where do they go when they slip away
As we sit beside them and pray?
Do they find the peace at last
That they dreamt about in the past?
What kind of journey do they endure
Perhaps they live on for evermore?
A second chance in another way
Just a different world and another day.
I guess it's only they who know
And we'll find out when we do go.
It's such a mystery to us down here
But I don't believe it's something to fear.
A chance to meet up with the past
To be with our loved ones at last.

J Robins